Published in (

The Anansi

www.anansiarchive.co.uk

Copyright remains with authors

All rights reserved.

This book or any portion thereof maybe not be reproduced without express written permission of the publisher except for brief extracts in reviews.

This anthology is entirely a work of fiction and any similarity to characters, descriptions and details portrayed is entirely coincidental. Any opinions herein are those of the author and not the publisher.

Cover: Yehor Lapko

Special thanks to Danni Jordan for

making this book possible

CONTENTS

Foreword..7

SHORT FICTION

SHOW ME WHERE IT HURTS

by Adam Lock………………...…………………….....9

JUST A FEW SECONDS

by Isobel Copley……………………………………….17

THE LIFE IT ONCE HELD

by Marcelle Creak……………………………………29

THY WILL BE DONE

By Rosie Christopher……………………………….34

THE THIRD CHOICE

Catherine Naisby……………………………..48

WILL YOU SEE MY MATE?

by Brian Hutchinson……………………………..54

LOOSE ENDS

by Sandra Morgan……………………………..….64

PENNY

by Emma Burnett……………………………………75

LUNATIC'S WOOD

By Atlas Weyland Eden…………………………….....81

LIME TREE ARBOUR

By Denarii Peters…………………………………….93

LEMONADE MEMORIES

by Rob Molan………………………………………..106

DEAD DREAMS

By Sandeep Kumar Mishra…………………....……….116

FOREVER I DROWN

by Kieran Rollin……………………………………..129

FLASH FICTION

THE PROPOSAL

By Anna Ross……………………………….....…..142

THE RELEASING

By Fiona Ritchie Walker……………………………….144

SECOND-BEST HUSBAND

By Chris Cottom……………………………………….146

VOICES

By R.F.Marazas……………………………………….148

TILL DEATH DO US PART

By Holly Hamp…………………………………………..150

A PATIENT LISTENER

By June Barnes-Rowley……………………………..…..152

READING IN WINTER

By David Davies……………………………………….153

POETRY

FULL MOON

By Junia Dia…………………………………….....…..157

COUNTERPOINT

By B.C. Burnett……………………………………….159

UNDERESTIMATED KNIFE

By Lydia Durrant…………………………………………...161

THE PHONE CALLS

By April Miller………………………………………………162

LETTER

By Max Williams……………………………………….....164

THE GARDEN

Lorelei Clarke……………………………………………..165

RAVEN ON MY SHOULDER

by Kim Tennison………………………………….……...167

LOVE IS A FALLEN DOVE

By Neeve Milsom……………………………………….....170

I SLEEP AND I SLEEP AND I SLEEP AND I

by Lewis Leverett……………………………………..…..171

DARLING

By Goda Buikute……………………………………….....173

A LETTER FROM PERSEPHONE

By Alexia Schauer………………………………………..175

THERE'S PEACE IN PROSPERITY

By Hannah Robinson-Wright...............................178

THE DISHES ARE CLEAN

By Eiman Anwar..180

GLANCING OVER PAPERBACKS

By Simeon Lumgair...181

FLYING ENVY

By Olya Carter..182

SPEAKING TO MY FATHER, SPEAKING TO MY MOTHER

By Luigi Coppola..184

AIRPORT SECURITY

By Charlie-Mai Dixon...186

SWALLOWED

By Imogen Smith..188

JASMINE

By Stephen Kingsnorth.......................................189

BUT YOU'RE STILL HERE

By Zara Shafique..191

Foreword

Current events can prove an inspiration to writers seeking new themes for their work and during the lifetime of The Anansi Archive, we have certainly lived through some profound world drama.

Earlier competitions have brought the Covid-19 pandemic into the minds of story-tellers and war in Europe was the focus for a number of entries into this Spring's competitions. But does the contemporaneous nature of the subject make it any more relevant as fiction? When seeking contexts for our prose, it is often the common themes that provide the most enduring fuel for our writing. Common, in the sense that they are shared by us all whether we come from Iowa or India. In that sense, they are neither displaced or rooted by a point in time.

Perhaps the timeliness of Covid or the Ukraine conflict actually rule them out for us as a context. We may need more distance from the subject in order to tell our story and for now it is something best left to reportage.

This collection reflects not so much timeliness but timelessness of themes and we convey it to you with acknowledgement at the measure of all our contributors endeavours and the success at their achievement.

Dave Jordan, Editor   July 2022

Short Fiction

SHOW ME WHERE IT HURTS

By Adam Lock

The great silence didn't happen all at once, so there is no definitive way to pinpoint when it occurred. It did, however, begin in my youth. It began when a linguist was interned in the prison of a hostile foreign power. Using only will, she discovered a way to communicate without words. To imprint an idea directly into another's mind.

Upon her release, she taught another this method of communication and thus it spread. For many, once they were shown how, the silence came as easy as breathing. For many more it was all but impossible. Countless people strived and toiled to find the silence, but by some cruel joke of fate or genetics, no one knows which, they found themselves incapable. Some resisted the pressure to find the silence, but it was after all an act of conscious, and an act of conscious can so often melt into unconscious. They would discover their inherent ability unwittingly and just like everyone else, once they started communicating this way they couldn't stop.

Eventually those who found the silence would only communicate through the mind and as such, they would only communicate with one another. Quite quickly it seemed, they forgot how to speak, then they lost their comprehension, then the ability to write, and then the ability to read.

What followed was lives running parallel. Two groups existing alongside each other, but intersecting minimally. The great silence split families. It made orphans and widowers in all but name. Yet those who found the silence were thankful for it. Everything was so much easier to them now. They either didn't recognize what they lost or they didn't care. There is no use dwelling on it as there is no way for us to ask and no way for them to tell.

I felt no such loss from the great silence but we all feel its impact in certain ways. When we're struck down with sickness and visit the hospital, we cannot describe our ailment to the doctor. Not all doctors could find the silence, but most did. Those that didn't, could no longer communicate with their colleagues and found their job untenable. Of course, when it came to their replacements, it was impossible for anyone who hadn't found the silence to be hired by those who had, and thus our hospitals are now exclusively staffed by doctors who communicate through the mind. Most high paying jobs have experienced something similar. We are able to point to the places that hurt but can't articulate our symptoms properly. They can still interpret numbers, create charts and graphs, they can still conduct their physical examinations and use machines to run tests and we often get better, but we seem to die in larger numbers each passing year. The doctors are searching blind without us properly prompting them and the nurses, who still communicate verbally and do most of the work, struggle to give the necessary care without proper guidance as to the nature of the illness. We don't have any statistics to back this up, as they are collected, collated, and interpreted by those who have found the silence, and they could never provide us with the appropriate context to judge them properly. But our parents die younger than their parents and our funeral clothes are wearing down to greying colours and fraying threads.

Meteorologists found the silence.

A massive storm swept over our shore a few years ago. They tried to warn us about its imminence and potential for destruction. They provided weather maps to our news stations, but were not able to properly articulate the enormity of what would take place. We watched our televisions as a news anchor tried but failed to properly interpret the danger. We saw the ominous ember passing over the digitalised topography of our island, yellow at its margins, then orange, then red, then purple at its centre. The eye of the storm passing directly over our city. For some this was enough and they boarded up buildings and evacuated. The Silent evacuated entirely of course, and for others this was enough signal to follow suit. But many stayed. To them this was just another instance of being left behind, and they felt they'd grown accustomed to that by now.

The storm arrived and brought with it havoc and fury. Unrelenting beads of rain fell from the sky and got caught up in the wind, thrashing against the sides of buildings and coating the air in a thick layer of moisture. A lot reached the ground; too much to permeate the concrete. It overwhelmed the sewage system and began to pool on the surface, deeper and deeper, as skies grew ever darker and the rain more ferocious. Waves were whipped and fish were thrown from the river onto land fast resembling their home. Soon the river broke its banks and more fish passed through, propelled by a strong, unforgiving current that ran through the veins of the city. People drowned in their basements and those foolish enough to be outside had the clothes ripped off their back by the flood that engulfed them. When I returned to the city, fish flailed in the gutter, as the last remnants of water washed away into the sewer and starved them of oxygen. Bloated bodies lay near formless at the side of the road, curled around traffic signs and street lights, like resilient barnacles revealed by the retreating tide. Their skin discoloured to the true purple at the eye of the storm.

These bodies were then replaced on street corners by preachers. Men in black hats, waving bells and placards, hollered about the rapture. They claimed that those who found the silence were God's chosen. That they shall inherit the earth and that we will toil and burn the way only sinners can, unless we can find a way to join them. Many were taken in by this sermon and soon there was an influx of men with shaved heads, wearing orange robes, followed by disciples who preached that they could help us find the silence—for a small fee of course. Motivated by desperation, people didn't question why the devout followers hadn't yet found the silence themselves, but most of these men were revealed to be frauds eventually. One such man was discovered when engaged in a circle of meditation. One of his clients knocked over a candle that set his robe aflame. His resulting shouts and curses, revealed him as an imposter, with a limited vocabulary at that. Eventually people melted back into a state of casual acceptance, as people so often do when confronted with the true nature of their powerlessness.

Life goes on. I spend my days cleaning the university in silence. The great minds that work here don't communicate with words and feel uncomfortable hearing ours. I often find myself holding my breath when I pass by them. They stand so still, the affectations that come with speech, that move arms and crane necks, are all but gone. Occasionally they may nod their heads in acknowledgement of a point I cannot hear, but mostly they are as still as statues. When I happen upon a full lecture hall, they resemble a mass of rigid trees, in a scene ironically so unnatural. They don't look at me, much like a tree wouldn't, and in this sense at work I become a trapped ghost routinely ambling about a haunted forest.

This isn't completely true. One man looks. He is the oldest of all the lecturers and seems to have a sentience the other trees lack. I like to think of him as the guardian of the forest—a Tolkien Ent. He often turns to see me as I walk by, and the action sends a shiver through my bones. It is disconcerting to be seen when you think yourself invisible.

There is a grand old library at the heart of the university. Books are packed into shelves from floor to ceiling and now rest abandoned, portals to different worlds, attempting to pull passers-by into their orbit but only succeeding at attracting dust. A dust which coats them, resting between their pages and decorates the spiderwebs clinging to the corners of the shelves. I have never cared for reading but it saddens me to see them this way. Entire worlds never to be explored. A life's work forgotten and discarded. I have taken it upon myself to clean this room shelf by shelf, ensuring each book is free from the grime and dirt that thrives in buried places. It is quite possible that by the time the room is complete, it will be time to begin again where I started. A certain hopelessness pervades this task, yet I feel compelled to complete it all the same.

The old lecturer recently stumbled upon me going about my work and he looked on for a few moments in what I believe to be disbelief. He then silently picked up a cloth and set to work on a shelf I hadn't reached yet. He couldn't ask what I was doing or why, but he mimicked my actions, parting the hardened back and cover, fanning the pages, and delicately shaking the book so dust wafted from the paper. He then took the cloth and wiped the spine, back, and cover, before delicately placing the books in a pile so he could clean the shelf. At first, he looked upon the pages as he dusted, but soon I noticed his effort to look anywhere else but there. We continued like this in silence, then parted in silence. He never came to help me again, but this was far from our last interaction.

I spend my evenings in the pub with fellow Speakers. The air is filled with our words and our breath meets the warmth to fog the windows. We tell each other stories and every other day a girl stands on a chair in the corner and sings ballads from a time before the silence. We only speak of current events within our sphere as Speakers, and never of advancements in medicine or technology, as how are we supposed to know of them. We see The Silent with new devices, but they could never explain how they are used. We are given new medicine when we visit the doctors but can only take it on faith. I suspect an inventor has found a way to transmit the silence for television frequencies, as they now have their own news channels, but there is no way of knowing for sure, and as such would only be a frustrating discussion.

A friend asked the other day, "Do you think The Silent have evolved beyond being human? We must be different enough to be separate species now. Most of the stuff we do the same, we share with say, dolphins. Some days I feel closer to a dolphin truth be told."

I replied, "That's some awfully clever sounding talk. You ought to be careful you don't find the silence, or worse yet become a dolphin."

Aye, stories, singing, and laughter is all we need. Plenty of laughter and plenty of drink. That's what this place is and how it will remain, barring the old lecturer's brief visit—the last time I saw ever him. I noticed him more and more after the library, then one day I found he was following me. He followed me from the university to the pub, then took his place alone at a table by the window. A girl stood on a stool in the corner and began to sing. She sang,

"She was lovely and fair as the rose of the summer,

Yet, 'twas not her beauty alone that won me."

The room chanted, "Oh no!"

" 'Twas the truth in her eye ever beaming

That made me love Mary, the Rose of Tralee."

I watched him for the songs duration and noticed as a tear ran down his cheek. What was hurting the man I'll never know. I have no way of asking and he can neither show nor tell.

Adam is a 26 year old writer of speculative fiction from Liverpool. He has a degree in English Literature and Creative Writing and an MA in World Politics. He loves writing that can take the unbelievable and make it seem everyday...or vice versa. Adam recently finished drafting his first novel and is about to begin seeking representation.

JUST A FEW SECONDS

By Isobel Copley

You turn off the car engine and sit for a few moments. You let your body sink into the quiet, taste a rare second of calm. The kids woke you nearly five hours ago. It's not even mid-morning. "Make the most of every minute" they say. "Time will go so fast" they say.

Double yellow lines but you've bumped up onto the grass verge beside the hedge. Easier to park here than struggle the extra yards up the hill with a toddler and a baby. You look over to the houses. Yawning windows, silent front doors, keepers of family secrets.

"Are we there mummy?"

Looking in the mirror you see your son's face, straining to get out. There is a crust of milk across his top lip. Flash of annoyance, how have you missed this?

You reach across the front seat for your bag. Your phone has slithered out. Stuffing it back in, you pull out your lipstick and slick it across your lips. You wish you'd had time to wash your hair. Butterflies dance in your stomach. One more glance in the rear view mirror. You open your door. A lull in the traffic. Take your chance while you can. This road is perpetually busy. You step out, hoisting the bag over your shoulder.

Damp, grey. Bare branches drip wet seconds. A solitary bird

chirrups overhead. You can't see it but its presence is somehow comforting. In the distance you pick up the hum of the dual carriageway. Deep breath. Earthy. Grounded. It might rain later. You hope you'll be home before then.

Only just past 10 but you're exhausted. Always exhausted. You know you will never get used to being woken at 5am. Baby birds with permanently screeching mouths. You hadn't expected resentment as part of the family package.

You've been putting this morning off. But your feeble excuses no longer stand up. Your in-laws mean well, so your husband tells you, but the clifftop they preach from is too high. Offhand comments pierce: 'I always left my babies to cry. Never did them any harm'. You will perch on the edge of the sofa, while the baby screams in her grandmother's stiff arms. Your little boy will stroke their old dog too hard, too long, too close to its gunky eyes and clever retorts will fail you. You will leave as soon as politely possible wearing a Failing Mother badge above your heart.

You open your son's door. Undo his seatbelt.

"Come on Jonny. Give me your hand. Let mummy help you out." His eyes are excited. He slides out of his seat clutching his plastic dinosaurs to his chest. Too many. One slips onto the floor. You sigh impatiently,

"Can't you just take one?" But his hands are too small to hold them all. He bends to pick it up. Another falls.

"Honestly, this is ridiculous. You know they have toys

inside." You are cross now. Why does he always have to be so annoying? The baby beside him watches intently, grinning, dribbling. You make a mental note to put more cream on her chapped chin.

You fold your hand round Jonny's as he clambers down from his seat and lead him round the back of the car onto the grass verge. Muddy. He slides around gleefully. His wellies leave perfect imprints. Your frustration now starting to boil, you grab his shoulders a little too roughly.

"Just stand still beside me while I get Evie out then we'll cross over the road."

You open the door and lean across the baby. She giggles happily, flapping her arms in your face, accidentally catches your nose. Your eyes water. Boiling over now, you push her arms down and fiddle with the seat clasp. It never opens easily. You hate it daily. Gritting your teeth you glance up.

Through the car window in a stretched second you see your little son, blue jumper, skinny legs, head down, running across the road. In the corner of your eye, hurtling towards him, thunders a speeding van. A predator charging his prey. It probably only takes a millisecond to stand up and react.

You are sure you see the terror on the face of the driver as he careers closer to that tiny running figure. You think you can see his eyes widen and feel his foot desperately pump the brake pedal. You think also, although you knew he was facing away from you, that you can see the determined look on your son's face as he charges for the other side of the road.

"Jonny!" You scream.

People will try to tell you time is linear. That sixty seconds make a minute and sixty minutes an hour. That there are 84,600 seconds every day and since time has been measured, that number remains the same. It doesn't stretch. It doesn't elongate. It doesn't change. But that morning time moves differently. In the same way that one raindrop rushes from heaven to the ground below while its twin nonchalantly saunters down a window pane, time melts and curves to fool convention and spin you into a parallel world. The universe looks just the same. The bird is still singing, the grass is still green but there are pixelated patches which will never, ever, become clear.

Can you call it a miracle? Your little boy turns, his head still down and runs back towards the verge. The van careers past.

Collapsing onto your knees on the wet grass you pull his skin and bone body into yours. You fall sideways against the car. He falls with you. You tremble, gripping him. He lets himself be squashed tightly into you. In those stretched moments you share the same fierce heartbeat. You are conjoined. Fused. Attached by an everlasting umbilical cord. His soft cheek is cold against yours, tinged with a chill from the brief run. You smell his shampooed hair, the cotton imprint of his pillow. Your nose tickles the curl of his ear. All there. Every part intact. He is yours. Still yours. Gradually you loosen your grip, move your hands up and down his arms. You cup his soft cheeks. The bird still chirrups on the branch above you.

Seconds tick once again. You look into his always enquiring

face and gently wipe the milky crust from his top lip.

"Good boy." You try to keep your voice still. "Now, hold onto me while I get Evie out of the car."

****

Your husband warned you he would be late home. Something to do with a team meeting. There's always a valid reason. You wonder sometimes if it's a deliberate ploy, that he just can't face the mess of baby bedtime. But today you need him. Today you have nursed the images of the morning. You have caressed them, stroked them, grown them, banked them in the vault of mother guilt. You now need to off load, to bathe in his sympathy.

Coffee with the in-laws had passed in a cotton wool numbness. You sensed their concern but excused yourself saying you felt a cold coming. Jonny was so good. He remembered to take his boots off by the front door, drank his glass of milk and busied himself prancing his dinosaurs across the carpet. You talked about schools, camping holidays and the price of petrol. You were outside your body, teetering on the precipice of normality.

You let your in-laws hold Jonny's hand back across the road. Let them hold open his door, clip him into his seat and hand him his dinosaurs one by one. You held the baby inside your coat then lifted her into her seat. They stood together waving as you drove off. You wished they'd just disappear.

The day slid on almost without you. You merely played out the moves. Whatever systems you might try to put in place were as fleeting as the head of a dandelion – perfect, fragile then gone. You need to tell him all this. You need him to help you build a fence around your dandelion patch.

You hear his key in the door. Jonny charges out of his bedroom and downstairs,

"Daddy!" He puts down his bag and picks up his son,

"Hey boy, what've you been doing today?"

"I'm a monkey, Grandpa says so. Let me dangle." Your husband opens his arms wide and Jonny dangles, arms clasped tight around his father's neck, legs kicking. They're both laughing. A flash of irritation. You know bedtime is hard work if the children are over-excited. He moves into the kitchen and tickles his baby girl who squeals with delight in her high chair.

You are right. It takes two stories and the promise of a third in bed with mummy in the morning till you're finally back downstairs. He's changed into his jeans. He's already poured his glass. You push yours towards the bottle,

"Yes please". This is adult time and adult time always begins with a glass of wine. It's become a habit but one you feel you deserve. It doesn't take much, just that first sip, maybe the second. Normally you feel the muscles in your neck, shoulders, chest relax. But not this evening. You walk to the fridge, pull out a ready meal. You don't meet his eye.

"How was your day?" Although you are desperate you don't want to leap in straight away. His turn first. Another sip of wine. He launches into detail about people you've never met, never will meet but who infiltrate your lives because of the effect they have on his day. You paint an interested look on your face while inside you are screaming.

You take the meal out of the microwave and divide it onto two plates. Conscience makes you tip a few salad leaves into a bowl with a handful of tomatoes. You sit beside him, always beside him, at the breakfast bar. You hesitate. He notices. His hand rests lightly on your thigh. Asks what the matter is. And in that single moment, with that casual prompt, the chasm on which you were teetering tears open so loudly you will swear you heard it. Falling in, you spill everything. You are airborne, releasing the terror, the guilt, the frustration, the resentment and the fear. You hope his arms are open wide to catch you. With your eyes on his face, you tell how you'd climbed so carefully out of the car. How you'd held Jonny's hand all the way round to the other side. How you'd reached in to release Evie and how in that split second, that half second, that stretched, elongated, time-stood-still second you nearly lost his precious son under the wheels of a van. His eyes glue to his plate. He doesn't turn to look at you. You're not sure if he has even blinked.

"I don't know how it happened."

He takes his hand from your thigh. His head is still down. Your blood pounds in your ears. You try to stem your waterfall tears with your fingertips. Too scared to leave your seat to grab a tissue. "I need some fresh air." He pushes back his stool. He turns his back to you. Walks into the hall and grabs his coat. He's out of the front door, pulling it closed behind him. Click. The air in the kitchen is silent but you sense every molecule in it is supercharged, chaotic. If turmoil is contagious, it has spread from inside your head into every room in the house.

The kitchen clock has a loud tick. Regular, relentless. You try to adjust your body to its rhythm. Breathe in. Hold for ten. Slowly release. Breathe in. Hold for ten. Slowly release. You stare at the uneaten food. Gulp back your wine.

It is nearly an hour later before you hear his key in the door once more. An hour that has undone something you thought so tightly knitted. You try to hold your feelings down, rising to meet him at the door just like Jonny a thousand hours before. You reach out your hand to touch his arm but he carries on walking past you. No smiles. No monkey business for you. You are hollowed out in your own home.

He goes into the kitchen. You hear the ping of the microwave as he re-heats his food and the scrape of the stool on the tiled floor as he sits down to eat. You wait five minutes that seem like five hundred until he has finished. Then the silken cord that tied you together on your wedding day pulls you into the kitchen once more.

"I don't understand how you could have let this happen. What on earth were you thinking? Jonny is only four years old yet you completely ignored him."

"It wasn't like that. I had him right beside me."

"Well you clearly didn't, did you?" He looks directly at you. His top lip tightly folded into his face. There is no wriggle room and no answer. Because he is right. Because for those few seconds you ignored your little boy. And in that heartbeat you nearly killed him. You know there is nothing you can say. You let it happen.

Tidal waves of shame and misery wash over you. There was a yesterday, a happy life-is-good yesterday but now there is today and today has crashed down. You hover beside him. You want to put out your hand to touch his arm, his shoulder, to run your fingers along his cheekbone to the tender skin behind his ear but your hand stays still. You know it won't be received. Touch has always been his thing, his love language. He needs handholding, hugs, skin on skin but now it is a language on mute. You know there will be no cuddling up on the sofa in front of the TV, head on his shoulder. He will not offer to make a cup of tea before bed or go to the children if one of them wakes. He will climb into his laptop and say he has work to do before tomorrow. The air will stay cold and you will sit alone in your misery.

You know he is more than angry, he is confused. The pedestal he places you on has been dislodged. You wonder if he has seen into you. Maybe it's a mask you've been wearing, this motherhood, this home-maker. Maybe it's slipped. Fear. Guilt. Failure. 'Let's have a baby' seems so long ago when neither of you could see into the future. You consumed self-help books as a ladder towards excellence. Feed the right foods, establish sleep patterns, put in boundaries. You were kidding yourself you had it sussed.

He has often said that to him you are perfect. You've wondered each time how he can think this but you've been happy to receive his adoration whilst secretly believing he is actually the perfect one. Now you're not so sure. Jonny is asleep in his bed. It was an accident that didn't even happen. Maybe it's him who has made the mistake. You would never have dared think this before.

He goes up to bed before you. He has not looked at you again all evening. You wait until you hear the flush of the toilet and the pad of bare foot-steps from bathroom to bedroom. The house is silent. You climb the stairs, follow his footsteps, toilet, wash, bed. His bedside light is already off. You undress, dropping your clothes onto the floor. The sheets are marble cold. You cannot warm yourself against his flesh. Clutching the edge of the mattress, you weep into your pillow.

In the morning he leaves the bed with the dawn chorus. You hear the wood pigeons coo-cooing outside the window. Always in pairs. He goes straight to the bathroom. Showers, dresses swiftly. Evie cries. He walks out of the bedroom, down the stairs.

"Your daughter needs you or is it her turn to be abandoned today?"

He is gone. You remain silent under the duvet. You are bruised. Empty.

Your day passes just as it has done for the last days, weeks, months, with the innocent unabashed love of your babies. But today you do not resent the tantrums, the spills, the time it takes to complete the simplest task. You sit with them on your lap reading their favourite books. You play dinosaurs with Jonny. He loves it. You melt into Evie's huge dribbly grins. Jonny hears his Daddy's key in the door just before bedtime and you assume a loving smile as he spins his children around before you take them up to bed. When you come down he has poured the wine for both of you. Now he looks straight at you. Now he pulls you close. Now he wraps you in his arms. You breathe him in. Minutes pass. You are fused together. He asks you how your day has been. You know he has moved on.

But you look at his face and you re-read it. You see judgement and self-righteousness where once you read appreciation and confidence. You see remorseless and patronizing where you read ambitious and helpful. You wonder what he reads in yours. Devotion? Or duty? What will you now admit to for fear of retribution? Will you cover your mistakes, disguise your fears and conceal your disappointments? Will you wonder when carefree left?

You cook his favourite meal, ham, egg and chips. You suggest another visit to his parents at the weekend. You even say the sorry you have been practising during the day. This evening you are entwined, insatiable.

But as you bury your shame, you bury a slice of happy ever-after. You are damaged. From now on you will assess his reactions. From now on you will question his judgement. From now on you will learn to keep secrets.

Isobel Copley has her head in the clouds. She likes it up there; she can play with words in her own time and with no restrictions. The few times she leaves the clouds she spends watching people, their eccentricities, peculiarities and interactions. She likes beaches, river-swimming and colour.

THE LIFE IT ONCE HELD

By Marcelle Creak

The bug latches to my earlobe with the pads of its feet tickling my ear. I barely feel it skitter inside. I wasn't planning to get the critter, but it's promised to rid me of the disease that's stolen my hearing. My son's persistent voice nagged me not to take the risk. He told me the critter would've saved him if it weren't too late. I haven't heard my son's voice since his death, but it's lively and bold in my memory as if he were my guardian angel.

My doctor fastens a timer to my wrist and warns me that I have an hour to go anywhere nearby. I can hear my favourite sounds as my hearing returns bit by bit.

I pack up my things so I can stop by the supermarket for a loaf of ciabatta bread and swing by the park afterwards.

My son and I used to feed birds at the park. Once the disease hit, it wasn't safe to visit anymore. My wife told me she could hear neighbours hack nasty cases of phlegm through our thin walls.

We stayed inside. We weren't able to feed birds before he passed.

Everything is a faint static in my ears as the sun bathes me with its friendly glow. No birds glide in the vast blue, but they're sure to smell the bread's aroma.

Starting down our old trail lined with yellowing grass, I remember teaching my boy how to call the birds. I'd lean over to my son and explain with a low voice that we can't yell for the birds or they'd startle away. You have to whistle, I'd say. Like this. I lick my lips and whistle that tune like I did to soothe my son in bed. There's no rustle in the trees, but gravel crunches beneath my feet.

The noise is faint, but it's there.

I take a chunk of bread and toss it to the ground, but not an ant scurries after the crumbs. I whistle again, but there's no response. There's a crisp crunch under my shoe as I plop down on a faded yellow bench. I lean down slightly and scowl at a potato chip bag for startling the birds that could've been eating my bread.

I leave the loaf sitting on the bench and ball up the aluminium bag, greasy residue coating my fingers slick with a sheen. The nearest trash can is across the park. I hike through the trees trying to imagine my son swinging on their splintering branches, but I know the branch would break.

His joy doesn't echo as it did when he hollered for all his jungle to hear. His spluttery whistles can't follow the harmony of chirruping birds and ribbiting frogs because there is no symphony.

This park was supposed to be a museum of my son's happiest days and my brightest memories, but has become a mausoleum of all the life it once held.

I toss the bag, satisfied before I notice the edge of the small pond ahead of me is littered with garbage. The water is perfectly still. I stand so the toes of my shoes barely graze the water.

The surface doesn't ripple with the life beneath waiting to shatter the silence. I take a pebble in my grip and skip it across the delicate surface, it skips three times.

It's all in the wrist.

The pebble plops in clean, sending ripples across the water till they reach land. I can't see any fish scatter through the mucky brown tinted water. No ducks break through the surface.

I kneel down and collect the plastic straws, gum wrappers, and soda cans, anything I could carry.

With all the promises of everything going back to how it was before the disease, I believed the critter in my ear was a true saviour of life. But it can't breathe fresh nutrients into the soil, rejuvenate the oaks, or make the grass fluffy and green again. This park's been dying for some time now, but it's staying strong just as my son did. The disease consumed him slowly. His immune system was holding on, but that special cure was too late to preserve what was left. His cheeks grew sullen, body tightened against his ribcage, each bone noticeably crawling under his ghastly white skin whenever he shifted.

A stuffy breeze sweeps through the park, but it feels like a wheeze in my lungs. The trees shake off shrivelling leaves before they could fall themselves. There's a filth in the air that tastes like someone's soggy, grease-filled leftovers squelching at the bottom of a bag.

I dart across the park collecting gum wrappers, zip lock baggies of goldfish, and uncover the tiniest patches of greenery. I grab an old styrofoam cup with a putrid liquid leaking through the bottom, a sourness catching my throat. My nose flares with a deep intake of breath I can hear so loudly, it startles me. I stumble back as the trash falls loose from my grip.

The timer on my wrist beeps.

The timer says I have five minutes to return, but I don't want to leave.

I can't.

I watched the sickness fester in my son. I have to save this park before my mind and memories of our long sunny days grow murky.

My son's voice pleads with me to stay.

"Remember when we'd lay in the grass and the sunset made everything look orange?"

The cicadas would start singing. He'd attempt to whistle along by blowing spit.

"Exactly."

The timer beeps at my wrist incessantly. I rip it off and chuck it into the trash. The alarm muffles as I collect more rubbish to bury the timer. Our strolls are already starting to feel like distant dreams.

Marcelle Creak (they/them/their) writes to find the right words and explore intriguing concepts. They've been writing for five years and hope to always be improving at their craft. They have decided to do this by creating a website to publish their work at http://creakschronicles337281317.wordpress.com/

THY WILL BE DONE

By Rosie Christopher

"Mrs and Mr Barron? The consultant will see you now."

Dr Scollin beckoned to the handsome couple from his doorway, smiling warmly. He could see that they were skittish, likely to bolt at any moment. Yes, these two would need a little grooming.

"So, your first child! Congratulations."

Stepping across the threshold, Adwin eyed the polished quartz walls of the office, evenly illuminated by blue spotlights. As the heavy door clicked shut, he noticed that there were no windows, giving the impression that they had entered a stone womb. Or tomb. With relief, he detected a steady waft of chilled air from some hidden shaft. It smelled vaguely of lemon.

"It's great to see you both again. The last time must have been at the sample clinic what, two months ago?"

"Even longer!" Erica replied, rolling out a chair for her husband before settling into her own. "Time seems to flow faster and faster these days." She looked at the older man expectantly, then caught sight of her reflection hovering on the wall over his shoulder. It had warped into an unbecoming version of herself. Turning towards her husband, she grasped his hand for reassurance. Their eyes met and he squeezed her fingers.

"Well, I've got to say, this is such an exciting time for us, what with all that possibility ahead".

"All that choice," simpered his wife.

"Choices," corrected the consultant, motioning towards the holographic logo in the corner. A hollow head, incubating a baby instead of a brain, gradually turned. "Choices mean freedom", pulsed the tagline beneath, in life-affirming green.

Erica nodded eagerly. "Yes definitely, choices. That's why we're on this journey of course."

Dr Scollin smiled reassuringly and reached for his computer. "I've noticed that both your DNA profiles contain coding that we've found to be most suited to enhancements; I think you are going to be well rewarded for your efforts here today." At this, the doctor noted with satisfaction, the wife flushed.

His fingers danced around the keyboard for a few moments, then he inclined the screen towards the couple. A pale mauve DNA strand was spinning slowly behind the outline of a sexless child while various symbols floated around its body. "This programme is loaded with your genetic blueprints. It will enmesh your choices into the model, in preparation. Then we'll look at dates for the big day."

"So clever!" Adwin gushed.

"Okay, let's start at the beginning so to speak. Shall we talk about the basics? Gender?"

Erica's heart gave a little flutter. She and Adwin had considered this at length, even typing out the pros and cons on the spreadsheet Adwin had thoughtfully created. "Girl," she stated unequivocally.

"Initially we thought boy," Adwin added. "Easier than girls, apparently. But then we don't know how long the world will even need boys, do we?" He gave the doctor a rueful, man-to-man look. "So a girl it is."

The consultant tittered politely. "Too true. Right, well that was straightforward. Now for talent. You can pick one area of giftedness or three moderate strengths. You've had enough time to consider the list?"

This discussion had been trickier, the debate bordering on outright conflict at times. Adwin felt it was essential for life chances that the child should excel at something creative, if only to beat the damnable AI at something. However, Erica had hotly argued, it was too risky to bank on one quality. Much better for the child to be well-rounded, have something to fall back on. A gaming discipline, for example. After all, VR surveyance was, besides the human lab-rat industry, one area of the employment market where real people remained indispensable, even if it was just to test-run the weird and wonderful habitats being endlessly trolleyed out by ever more desperate tech companies; the Quasiverse had turned out to be overrated and riddled with anomalies. Sometimes even breaches. Opinion polls showed the populace to be inclining towards reality in an alarmingly increasing rate, wrecked though the true world was.

"There are still pockets of beauty out there," Adwin had whined. "Our child prodigy could contribute to that. Humanity could admire her creative endeavours long after we were gone."

Eventually Erica had her way: three strengths, but Adwin got to choose two. Philosophy and art. Erica had scoffed, regarding both as superfluous in a dog-eat-dog world. She opted for Data Science. "Humans drop data wherever they go," she'd lectured. "Data means dollar, and that's never going to change."

The appearance menu had been easier to agree on. Both wanted their progeny to inherit their amalgamated features. After all, few could afford reprogenics, which was even more extortionate than germline engineering; with their daughter resembling them, most people would not suspect the boost that she had been given pre-utero.

In a break from heredity, both had opted for speedy metabolism – what greater freedom could they afford their child than that of eating with impunity, Erica had quipped, while mournfully eying her husband's paunch.

"A1 vision, please." This particular option had been an extra - on time-limited offer - and although eyesight was easily correctable, they'd both heard horror stories of unfortunates returning from the laser with dry eye. "And no predisposition for cancer or mental health issues." This was another extra, with significant financial implications. They'd felt held to ransom by the price-tag, but privately Erica was worried that as they had chosen not to trust Nature, in turn Nature might be out for karmic revenge, so she'd insisted on them stumping up.

"Okay, diet proclivity next. Meat-eater, pescatarian, vegetarian or vegan? Or even raw."

Erica sat up. "Vegan. Not to avoid the meat-tax," she added hurriedly. "We're just doing our bit for the planet, aren't we Adwin".

The consultant hummed his approval and inputted their choices. "Sport now. You can choose one aptitude."

Erica rolled her eyes at her husband's nostalgic expression, smiling indulgently. "Adwin wants horse-riding. He's hoping we'll have to ditch the self-drives one day!"

Adwin tutted in mock-irritation. "No, I just love horses! Our girl will have her first pony by the time she's four." He looked at Erica pointedly. "Won't she! And it's not just horse-riding, Erica. You make it sound so underwhelming. It includes dressage and horseback archery."

"Good choice. And actually, our third most popular!"

There was a pause while the data organised itself into a human-to-be. Gradually the person icon on the screen started to fill, to indicate to the customer the percentage of possibility that had so far been determined. The line stopped at a mere eight percent. They had yet to navigate the complex mesh of genes that would create a desirable temperament, with an array of delicate balances to consider: childhood obedience versus adult self-assuredness. Humour versus sensibility. Innovation versus conformity.

"Here's one that always causes a bit of discourse," offered the consultant. "Kindness versus egocentrism. You read the guidance on this?"

It was another area where the couple had disagreed. Adwin felt certain that kindness was the root of happiness, citing the famously happy Tibetan Monks of Bhutan. Erica, on the other hand, had grown up in a one-car household, and had not been afforded her first Smartscreen until she was ten. She understood the stress of money troubles. "I want her to be driven," she had declared. "Focussed. You don't get ahead by being kind."

Adwin sighed. "We've agreed 50/50," – he gave her a sideways look – "though I would have gone for 90% kindness, personally. If our child becomes a dictator, we'll know who to blame."

"Nothing wrong with a benign dictator," she sniffed.

And so the afternoon wore on; the little person on the screen gradually filled as the seemingly infinite possibilities were honed and mapped onto a life path that would surely afford their offspring the best chances of a happy, successful life, free from the constraints of hardship, uncertainty and wrong choices. When the icon was at eight four percent, the consultant sat back. "Okay, we're getting there," he stated. "Now we just need to talk about permissions."

This was a new feature, "permissions" being a sanitised euphemism designed to strip the modified human of the ability to be foolhardy. It had been added to the reprogenics programme only two months ago but was already one of the most talked-about advancements of science on social media. Erica and Adwin felt lucky to be able to take advantage of such a safety measure, which surely any parent would opt for, given the opportunity. "We definitely want the full shebang," Erica declared. Adwin swung his head in an exaggerated gesture of assent. "Absolutely! I couldn't bear it if our daughter turned to drugs. So life-limiting!"

"Or worse," prompted his wife. "Imagine her running off with some infertile nonstarter!"

The consultant cleared his throat. "Okay, drug-blocker. But" – he looked up – "you are also opting for the whole shebang, as you put it?"

Erica tried to read the consultant's impassive features and was relieved to find no sign of reproval; modifying sexual preferences was a controversial leap in genetic engineering. With growing infertility, sperm banks had run dry. Following the introduction of tax breaks for fecund families, some parents were openly banning their children from same sex relationships, with many insisting on pre-nuptial fertility testing for suitors. Then there were the traditionalists who were vehemently opposed to such meddling, arguing that it was a basic human right to choose a partner from whichever gender they were attracted to, fertile or not. The Reprogeneticists had got round this by identifying the relevant set of genes and removing same-sex attraction in the first place, but such a bold move was still only endorsed on the QT. Even more divisive was the practice of engineering the propensity of a female to be attracted solely to more masculine types, to minimise the possibility of choosing an infertile man. Deep voices and heavy facial hair only, please. Testosterone had been rapidly losing out to oestrogen in the hormonal battleground of every man for generations now. After all, plastics had wrought havoc in all corners of the natural world; sperm quality was just another casualty. It was every parent's dread that little Johnny's balls would fail to drop, and he'd be cursed with a squeaky voice. Those were key giveaways. Some parents were even paying for voice box cosmetic surgery, but it was only a half-fix, and it was easy to spot a modified voice.

The consultant's attention returned to the keypad. "Complete package," he said knowingly as he ticked the option, discreetly coded 'H2T'.

There was a rumour that some of the maverick start-ups were offering race preferences as an under-the-table option. Adwin was disgusted that anyone should care about the colour of skin that their child went for, and even pointed out that mixed race children were renowned for their beauty. Secretly, Erica was disappointed that they had gone to a reputable clinic.

While Erica signed the relevant consents and authorised the next payment, Adwin gazed about the imposing office and his dreamy eyes fell upon an incongruous depiction of a dragonfly hovering over a lily, discreetly etched into the stonework above the door. It struck him that he had only ever seen either in the Quasiverse, and he wondered what a lily smelt like in real life. On the way out of the clinic, he asked his wife to name the sweetest scented flower she had ever come across. She looked at him strangely. "That's not a question I was expecting," she said. "But probably a rose. Why? What's yours?"

Adwin sighed. "I can't even remember. Anyway, let's go home."

****

In the evening they decided to celebrate in front of the cleanfire with a nip of vintage brandy, perhaps Erica's last before pregnancy. As she swirled the amber liquid around her glass and inhaled the spicy aroma as Adwin had shown her, he uploaded their chosen profile, a read-only version of which had been endowed to them at the clinic. Erica settled back into the silky sofa, infinitely more indulgent than its Quasiverse counterpart. As a rule of thumb, they tried to stay in the Realworld outside of work hours, as both agreed it kept them more grounded. In truth they were among the few who could afford a home whose luxury was not surpassed in a virtual habitat, so it was hardly a sacrifice.

Erica took a generous sip from her crystal glass then carefully set it down on the antique coffee table. "Adwin, when you've uploaded her, can you just project the data rather than the images too? I'm not sure I want to see what she'll look like, yet. What do you think?"

"Well, I know what you mean. It would be nice to keep an element of surprise. Tell you what, I'll password-protect the imagery. Hopefully I won't give in to temptation."

One by one each of their choices blinked to life on the display panel, word format only, and with furrowed brows they stole glimpses of the future. "At least we won't need to worry about vetting her crushes," Erica chuckled.

"True," agreed Adwin. "I wonder who she'll bring home," he wondered aloud. "Some top-grade jock, no doubt."

"God, I remember some of the awful types I used to hook up with," recalled Erica in a wistful voice. "I drove my mother mad. One even had a horn piercing in his brow!"

"No real bad girls for me, but I slept around a lot. Typical teenage boy, I guess. At least girls aren't like that. Not nice ones, anyway."

"Adwin!" Erica chided. "Don't be so old-fashioned! Boys shouldn't be promiscuous either! Well anyway, as long as the boy she dates hasn't been around the block. Goodness, I've just thought: we opted for pro-masculine attraction. He'll be awash with testosterone!"

Both were quiet for a while, each contemplating nightmare scenarios of their little girl in floods of tears over some two-timing player or worse, infected with a horrible sexually transmitted disease. The sudden realisation of this potential unintended consequence was unsettling.

"Still, it's good that she won't be able to try drugs," Erica soothed, sipping her brandy.

"Thankfully," agreed Adwin. Though I had great fun during my various forays into the world of substances. Some of my best childhood memories involved me being high as a kite!"

"You rebel!" scolded Erica. "You've never told me this!"

Adwin continued, full of nostalgia now. "There was this one time, my mate had grown some magic mushrooms, you know the modified ones that got the law changed again. Anyway, he snuck some spores into Guatemala when we went travelling and they sprung up all over the place! The parties we had on those bad boys. For a while, we were the most popular tourists in the jungle!"

Erica was not to be outdone. "Well I've got a confession. I snorted raw alkaloid once, and spent the night helping my mate to hack into JJ Jackson's Quasiverse. Remember the singer? We were in stitches.

"Then I spent the next six months petrified that some government bigwig would be at the door to arrest me! The things we got away with. Lucky my poor parents were none the wiser."

"Ah, how stupid we were. Funny enough, my magic mushroom buddy ended up using his entire inheritance on founding a tech school in Africa. Said the psychedelics had left him too enlightened to need material wealth!"

Erica snorted. "Well thank goodness our daughter won't be doing anything so hasty as that. Not with all our checks and balances."

"Yeah."

"Glad we included late onset puberty."

"Me too."

A silence fell over them as they each gazed into the dancing e-flames, lost in uneasy thought. Every now and then one of them would glance at the list of attributes they had cooked up for their daughter. How perfect she'd be. Utterly without fault.

"Adwin, do you think teenage rebellion has a developmental purpose?"

"Why, do you think that she might end up a has-been or something without it?"

"I don't know, yes maybe. Or just not, you know, complete."

Adwin considered this. "Well, I'm not sure about all that, I'm no expert. But I do know I had some exciting times as a rebellious teen. Happy memories I wouldn't swap for the world."

"But that's what we've done for her, isn't it. Swapped her world for one we've chosen."

"No, I disagree. We've bought her freedom from heartache, that's all."

She looked down. "At the price of her free will."

"She'll thank us, love, I expect. And anyway, not every teenager rebels. Plus, adolescence is only a tiny bit of a person's overall lifespan, and definitely the most dangerous bit. We're just preserving her from some of the worst possibilities. She'll still be fundamentally free".

"Oh yes, because when she's twenty she'll be able to choose a mate," she said sardonically. "As long as he's manly."

The uncertain flames flickered blue-green. "I wonder what our natural child would've been like. Randomly impregnated. It's mind-boggling that sex one day would produce a completely different baby to sex the next day."

Erica suddenly sat forward and grinned at her husband. She pointed upstairs, in the direction of their four-poster bed. "Fancy finding out what today's might be like?"

Adwin caught her eye and nodded decisively. "Do you know, Mrs Barron, that's the best idea you've had all day!"

Erica met his knowing gaze and laughed. She swigged the last of her brandy, motioning for Adwin to do the same. As he drained the last it, he shuddered and made a face. For a moment he remained in the thrall of the Smartscreen, but his reverie was broken when he saw that Erica was nodding at him in encouragement from halfway up the stairs. "So, what are we waiting for?"

Resolved, he leaned towards the display and, with a dramatic tap on the screen, he extinguished their ideal child, before following her up.

Rosie Christopher is a probation officer who has worked with a multitude of adults and young offenders over the years, giving her plenty of inspiration but not enough time to write! This is her first published work. She loves walking in the nearby New Forest in Hampshire, UK with her family and dog.

THE THIRD CHOICE

By Catherine Naisby

Scars? Yeah, I got scars. Comes with the territory. Some you can see. But the bad ones, no you ain't gonna see them, sometimes you get to see a bit of bruising, but the real scars, they go deep into your soul. And once you got them, you see them right away in anyone else. Taylor, she had them. Obvious. I knew right away. Her Mom did too, and I reckon I can guess why. Just proves my point.

Let me introduce myself. Name's Cora, I carry a .357 Smith & Wesson, live in the Bay Area, got a couple of rooms, one's the office. That'll do. That's all you need to know.

So this morning, there was a knock on the door, and this woman comes in, obvious druggie, but doing her best. I thought she was alone, but there was a kid lurking behind her, faded, almost translucent. Mom grabs the kid, pushes her towards me.

"Go on, Taylor," she said. "Show her."

Taylor was scrawny, fourteen, maybe younger. Mom lurched forward, pulled up her dress. The bruises were fading, but still distinct: finger marks, inside upper thigh. That's the visible part. You can guess the rest.

"Well?" she said, staring hard at me.

"You been to the cops?"

"They took one look at us."

She didn't need to say any more. I named a fee.

"Jesus!"

"I'll need a deposit."

I'd lose my licence if I didn't charge a fair price.

She handed me some bills; crumpled, stained. Said she had to get back to work or she'd lose her job. I knew there was no job, only what the cops had seen.

I said, "Okay, leave Taylor with me. I'll take her for a drive, see if she knows the place."

I knew where it would be.

She nodded, suddenly in a hurry to leave. "Taylor? You be a good little girl now." She looked round my shoddy little office, jealous. "You be good." More tenderly.

"Come on Taylor."

"Yes Miss."

"It's Cora."

I knew she wouldn't.

The car was a few blocks away, near my sister's place, so we walked through the park. I told her we needed to pick up my nephews first, twins, eight years old. My sister likes to be rid of them for an hour or two. She knew I'd be on a case, but anything for a bit of quiet.

We get days in the Bay when it starts hot, and it gets hotter, and this was one of them, with the sort of sun that weighs down on you so heavy you need to get drunk or high or be in love, proper love. The park was full of kids walking together, boy-girl-boy-girl, swishing through the sunlight. I could've been like that once. Maybe Taylor still could.

There was an old man, wet lips, loping along the gravel. He saw us, averted his eyes. Taylor didn't react. That narrowed it down.

The sun bounced back in hot waves from the beach. We got to my sister's apartment, and the twins were all grins and "Auntie Cora!"

They knew the drill, we'd done this often enough before. Back out into the heat, and there was this big Buick, stopped at the lights, dark man driving like in the movies, drawing on his cigarette. No reaction from Taylor. The lights changed, the man put his foot on the gas. The twins were bouncing, excited by the roar of the engine, but they were on elastic, they always bounced safely back. We crossed the road.

"Here," I said. Taylor's eyes widened when she saw my wreck of a car. I filled it with my fake family: teenage daughter, twin sons. Felt good. Taylor sat in the front, bright, vivid in the sun, almost beautiful. I used to look like that.

We passed two men with dark briefcases—I knew it wasn't them, but I asked anyway to get her used to the question before it mattered.

Marina Way, and I turned into a parking lot. Taylor was reluctant to get out of the car. The boys were yawning in the back with the heat. I found some candy in the glove compartment, handed it back.

"Don't open the door to anyone," I said. They knew the drill. I'd take them to the pictures later. Worth ten minute's wait in a hot car.

Me and Taylor got out and walked behind this woman—or maybe it was a man. I looked at Taylor. She shook her head.

Then she stopped, stared hard—a cripple, amputee, gripping his crutches, dirty hat brim covering his eyes. Someone worse off than her? She nearly came alive. A couple crossed the road, his hand on her shoulder, proprietorial, pushy. Taylor crept closer to me, gripped my hand. A tennis court, couple in the hot sun, him shouting, her pulling away, scared, the oppressive buildings around them. The man raised his fist.

Taylor whimpered. We were close.

A blisteringly hot corner, deep shadowed path—I wanted to get out of the heat, but it led back to the beach, wrong way. We kept going. This was it. White walls. I remembered a black eagle tattoo, rings, a huge body like a wedge; a dark carpet, stinking, burning.

I looked at Taylor.

"It's okay," I said. "I know."

We waited in the shade. A man went in, but he couldn't see us. I kept telling her whenever anyone went in or out: "They can't see us, we're not here."

The poster on the wall: Totally NUDE and lower down, a label: Fire sprinkler control valve in basement 3/2 Columbus West Side.

A different man came out; huge, broad, muscled back like a wedge, tattoos—a black eagle, seven rings.

Taylor was shaking.

"C'mon. Back to the car," I said, and I dragged her away. She could barely walk.

The twins were asleep, empty candy bag between them, wrappers everywhere. I locked the doors, ran my fingers down the faded scars on my arms, the ones that didn't mean much, the ones that were a distraction to hide the darkness underneath.

"You have a choice," I said.

I took the .357 out of my purse.

"The rings on his back—think of them like targets. You know how to shoot?"

She shook her head. "Get close enough, you don't need to know. That's choice number one."

I put the gun in her lap, and it sat there, huge, heavy.

"Choice number two. Pretend the gun's a popsicle, put it in your mouth. Then you never have to be like your mom, you never have to shut your ears and eyes, never have to be a drunk, never have to be like me, nobody can hurt you ever again; one small burst of hurt like fireworks, like the most beautiful thing you've ever seen, ever felt, and then nothing."

We sat there for a long time. The sun was going down, it was cooler.

"Those are your choices," I said.

"No." She croaked the word out at last.

One last choice. The third. The .357 lay heavy between her skinny thighs. I picked it up, felt the warmth of it nestling in my hand, a slight itch beneath, like a scar that refuses to heal.

"Keep an eye on the twins," I said.

Catherine Naisby lives in North-East England, reads widely, and takes her inspiration from many sources, both literary and artistic. Her publications include two poetry collections, five novels and a Holocaust memoir, as well as numerous short stories and poems in journals such as Aesthetica, Crannóg and Ambit.

WILL YOU SEE MY MATE?

by Brian Hutchinson

The entries between the wee houses on the Woodstock and the ones on the Castlereagh Road were full of joy and wonder if you were under ten years of age. There were bins to kick, derelict houses to hide in and back doors to pee against. If you were between thirteen and seventeen, cigarette's where hidden on roofs, cider was buried beneath old sofas and there was always a short cut from over keen R.U.C patrols.

The Cregagh, had not one entry unless you stretched a point and included behind the shops at Greenway, everyone knew they were just the back of the shops. You couldn't count the wider ones on the upper Cregagh Road round Theipval. They had bushes, trees and occasionally grass. A real entry should be narrow enough to touch both sides with your hands outstretched. The ground should be uneven and full of building debris, bricks, and wood.

Most of all an entry had to suggest more, more than seemed probable and always more than what you believed was possible. An entry was a bit like the Tardis from Doctor Who. Apart from the deceptive space issues you had to be aware of the Monsters and their Minions who lurked within. An unwary boy could fall victim quick enough.

Between the ages of thirteen and seventeen my twin loves of cider and erections had fought for dominance on a weekly basis. This was no more so than when walking through one of the entries at the bottom of the Woodstock. Our H.Q was the first derelict house behind Wilton the Funeral Parlour at the top of Hatton drive. For two or three years, this was very much the preferred location but we roamed as far down as the Munchman Chipper and as far up as Russell Cellars Off Licence at Ardgowan Street. We would cross to the King Richard Bar or Centre Spot Club on the Castlereagh Road. Technically we shouldn't have been here at all. This was the Woodstock or the Castlereagh and we were The Cregagh!

The pull of the entries was such that we would risk a run in with Maffa and Jeff or any of the other "half a heads" for a wee play up the entry. There were maybe eight or nine Cregagh Boys in total who came down to Hatton Drive. Three of us more so than others. Wando, Billy and me. Robert Wilson, Stephen McFarland, Ski, Buff, and Craig were good attenders, but they were more community center guys. There was a guy called Bishy who lived near Wyse Buys, so he was neither Woodstock nor Cregagh. He was neither Woodstock or The Cregagh but girls gravitated towards him, and it would have been rude not to have helped him out with his "wee over attraction problem".

Monday to Friday I would do the least homework I could get away with from 4.30pm to 5.30pm. I had decided early doors that neither the Ma nor the Da would ever see any correspondence from Annadale. This served me fine until the school posted a letter about parents evening on the one day, I was genuinely sick and couldn't simply take a copy home. The Ma had the letter, her best coat on and was standing in front of a range of second form teachers explaining that my migraines were muchly improved and that they should expect an immediate improvement in my performance. If my migraines were immediately improved after that Thursday night, my legs tolerance to a well swung feather duster certainly wasn't. Still, that was in the future. Homework complete by half past five and I was out of my school clothes and into my jeans and T shirt. If I could find a shoe with a point to it that was great. If I could find a suede one with a point and maybe a buckle or zip and that was better. If a zip, buckle, patent leather and a point could come together my world was bliss.

Once I was changed, I would fire my tea into me as fast as I could. Normally to a chorus of "slow down wee lad" from my Da or the sisters keen to get my Ma in a rage would keep a running commentary of "Our Brian's not chewing at all, Our Brian is eating with his mouth open, Our Brian is gulping it down". I could never understand if they were so quick to lay claim to "Our brain" why they took such delight in "Our Brian" getting walloped the way I did. The tea would come with a drink, normally milk, and two slices of bread and butter. There were always chips, mash and roast potatoes were Saturday only and there was no pasta on savoury rice in number forty-five until 1984.

Along with the chips there was either, Heinz Baked Beans, Bigga Marrowfat Peas or Heinz Spaghetti Hoops. A rotation system was in operation but all three were totally acceptable. These would be paired with sausages, fish fingers, beef burgers (no baps), vegetable roll, stewing steak, mince and onions or my favourite Fray Bentos Steak and Kidney pie. Regardless of the tasty combination I would have my Levi

Jacket or Two-Tone Jacket on by 550pm and be stepping down the path heading for the entry at Hatton Drive. During term times, this was a Tuesday and Thursday night as Monday and Wednesday were after school rugby training. Friday and Sunday where possibilities with Saturdays reserved initially for The Cregagh Community Centre Disco, then Robinsons, Washington, The Liverpool, Kelly's and eventually Lavery's.

We didn't really "call for each other" the way girls did but you knew what time Wando or Neilly would set off from their house at and most times you could modify your pace so that by Bells Bridge or Daddy Winkers turn off at worst you have exchanged an "All right" and fallen into step. As you got as far as Ardgowan Street you would always cross to be on the side of the Off Licence. A wee look up the entry here was always worth it in case there were bottles that had been put out because they "weren't right" or once the store gate was left open and Stephen McFarland got in and out with two crates of Harp. Nothing was really said until Ardgowan street other than the normal schoolboy teasing about football. "Chelsea are all shit hawks like." Sometimes it was hard to defend logic when it was put to you no matter how much you loved the Blues. They were pretty much that from 1978-1984.Everyone else followed United or Liverpool but I had Chelsea. Thanks for that Micky Droy, Cheers.

We would check back doors and chase young kids with sticks as we weaved the entries until we were down by Hatton. It would normally be just after seven. Wando would break out the regal and him and me would smoke while Billy just stood and combed his hair. If a teenage girl would walk past regardless of looks a chorus of "Give us yea" would crack the air followed by the same girl(s) either giving us the fingers or shouting, "bum boys" either of these meant one of us was in with a chance but we didn't know which one of us nor did we know which one of them was interested. Silence was the enemy. The silent ones never came back. I was convinced the silent ones became Nuns or were Lizzies or possibly Lizzie Nuns. Olive, Anne, Elaine, Angela and Suzie all lived near Hatton and would go to the Community centre disco. Olive and Anne lived in the drive. All or at least most of them would put in appearance at some time as would some of the other Cregagh regulars. There were no boys from the Woodstock who hung about here, they were further down at the pool room across from the Munchman or at the entry over by the King Dick. Although we got on well it was still worth being careful. The love between the Cregagh and the Woodstock wasn't always so noticeable.

When a group of girls passed for a second time the shouting would become a little bolder and more direct. "Oi, Blondie want me to keep you warm." "Big girl your arse is chewing a toffee." "Mon over I've got a big surprise honey." The responses where the same despite the suaveness of The Cregagh boys. A middle finger with a wee dance of the shoulders or a witty comment. "Come on back when your voice breaks, and your balls drop!"

As they passed out of sight, we would divvy them up. "Wando the wee Blonde is yours, the ginger one's mine." Billy would be irate straight away and, on his feet, animated. "Hold on why do I get the wee boot with no Tits." Finger pointing. It would wind him up most if you blew smoke at him and simply said. "Gingers get last pick and Your Ginger!" This was always funny. Once some negotiation had taken place we would agree who was taking who were.

"Wando, you can take the Blonde up the entry at Hatton, Billy you've the entry at Willowfield Church and I'm having the house." Near violence would erupt as the derelict house was your best chance of slipping the hand or getting a feel. There were two old sofas in the house and it didn't smell much. The allocation of the house was normally on a rotation basis but if you were seeing a girl more than twice you got priority.

At this stage, all sexual adventures were communal. If one of us got lucky and got a feel or slipped the hand it counted for us all so if the case was strong enough regarding a second date or simply a well-known rumour that the girl in question was a dirty bit, a Cregagh Boy was bound to step aside to offer his mate the best chance. Just because we had a well-developed protocol of allocation of girl and location didn't mean that things were seen that way by the girls of the Woodstock.

Once the regulars, Olive, Anne, Elaine, Angela and Suzie appeared that was often enough to ensure that the others would never return. Olive despite her 4ft5inches height had a way of crossing her arms across her huge chest and stepping forward that would set the other Woodstock girls to flight and immediately lesson the pressure in my wranglers.

Olive though did play a useful roll once she decided she was "seeing Wando" as this effectively left more options for us.

Olive decided she was seeing Wando. He didn't get a say. I wasn't there the first night but she simply took him by the hand and lead him down Hatton drive and into the House she shared with her cousin and her Auntie.

He wasn't asked. No one spoke on Olives behalf. She simply took him away and that's the way it was for at least another

twenty years. Wando still hung out by the derelict house at the top of Hatton. He still drank his quarter bottles of Bacardi or Vodka. He still sang Dexy's or the Pretenders and would occasionally chase of other boys and get in a fight or two but when all 4ft5inches of Olive took him by the hand he would walk quietly down that wee street and into the two up two down. That was just the way it was. They would scream, fight roar and bawl. They would slap each other and occasionally he would walk off with another girl but when Olive reached out and took his hand he would quietly follow. Boobies were powerful things!

After a second pass, if the girls were still interested and Olive hadn't frightened them of, or to be more accurate had only frightened of the ones that Wando was interested in or that she knew were interested in Wando. Then they would come over and stand by us. We would immediately ignore them. If other Cregagh Boys arrived at the derelict there would be a quick reallocation of girl and locality by us but no chat at all. Once we were clear that they had been ignored properly The Cregagh Boys would head of alone leaving the regular girls, Olive, Anne, Elaine, Angela and Suzie, with the new girls. Sometimes when we came back they were all gone or partially gone. We never questioned what had happened. Girls were great but we were still teenage boys and the entries had other attractions. So often we left them at the corner we would explore. Dares would be set for climbing onto the back walls and balancing before walking along giving a commentary of what you could see in the two up two down houses. Ski was up one night and it was pretty much the normal stuff, "They are having a chippy tea, Footballs on the Tele, no one in" always just the headlines before walking carefully on along the six-inch-wide wall. The most anyone had managed before an angry householder was out hurling abuse or potatoes was twelve back windows.

Ski stopped at four. "Aww Fuck me. Budgie get up here, Billy you to. "Aww Fuck me!" His voice was quiet but excited as he hunkered down to get a better view. "Jesus Christ, would you look at that." Billy and I were back down the entry and quickly up on the wall. We were quiet and quick as a cat policing a mouse. "What, what is it." Billy was first to hunch down." Fuck." I was down just a second after and all three of us could hardly believe it.

A very large naked fat man was being hit on the arse with a cane by an even larger naked fat woman. She was really swinging it and because the living room lights were on with each stroke you could see both his and her fat flesh jump and quiver. "Dirty, Dirty, Fuckers." Ski whispered. There was no arguing with that as she crashed another stroke against his arse. "In the living room with the fucking football on. Sickos.SIckos. SICkos.SICKOS........." Ski was up and dancing then Billy, then me. All three of us were chanting and holding our groins. They slowly turned. She ran for the back door and suddenly the yard was full of angry fat flesh and it just wasn't as funny. We were of as a bamboo whipped at the air. "Came here back to me you skitter." Not likely and not often the entry offered up such reward. We were down of the wall and buying sweets on the Castlereagh Road as innocent as could be.

The pool room where the Woodstock boys hung out was another Cregagh Boys only trip. The entry at the back of here was rumoured to be where the UDA would take you if you were due a battering. It was the only entry totally of limits. That was probably why there was no hassle in the pool hall. It only had two tables and it was winner stays on.

It had two poker machines and two fruit machines and no staff. It smelt overly of bleach despite the smoke. We all had lots of conversations about robbing the machines but no one wanted taken up that entry so we played our pool, lost our money to the U.D. A's poker machine and bought a pasty from the Munchman before taking it to the entry's down by the London bar. A bit like Ardgowan street it was always worth a look, a drunk with a carryout would often set his carryout down to piss against an entry wall and forget to pick it up. You'd never know unless you looked. Once back at the corner of Hatton Drive and the Funeral Parlour we would wait to see what had happened. If there were none of the new girls left, then it was a night of smoking and banter. Only Wando and Olive and sometimes Bishy and Anne ever "went with each other" the rest of us just talked and slagged them. There was never only one new girl. For it to work that had to be at least two. Timing was everything. The normal banter would flow and then one of the new girls would slowly walk up the entry behind the derelict house and keep walking until she was at the very end where she could neither see nor hear or hear and see. The atmosphere would change. All the girls left, new and old would be in on it and the boys would know nothing.

Your mouth would dry and if you had a regal you'd smoke it. Even on a cold night you could feel your armpits moisten. Conversation was stilted. Whichever new girl was left would walk towards the Woodstock but first would softly say "Budgie come here to I ask you something." Then everyone would know it was you. You'd follow her until the others couldn't here and then shed ask "Will you see my mate? "If the answer was yes, she would give you details of which entry to meet at and either a time for later that night or more likely the next night. Then you would both walk back together to the derelict house. If the answer was no, you would both walk back together to the derelict house. The girl would walk of down the entry to find her mate and tell her and conversation would return as normal. If there had of been more than one new girl still left the process would repeat. Only when all the new girls were gone did anyone ask. "Well, what did you say?"

It's hard not to feel that the PlayStation generation should not spend just a little more time in an entry.

Born in East Belfast in 1965 Brian has always written "wee stories". Looking at the people around him, hearing their triumphs and struggles keep him writing. Wee stories matter.

LOOSE ENDS

by Sandra Morgan

And now Julia felt able to slow down. She'd given them the slip again.

She threw her head back and gulped in lungfuls of salty air. The sea spray felt soft as cobwebs on her lips.

Before her lay the gloriously empty, misty expanse of beach. Out-of-season. The best time. No visitors with screaming kids and striped windbreaks and yapping dogs. The only sign of life was a squat, black taxi pulling into the distant parking area behind the deserted lifeguard's hut.

When the taxi's back door opened, the figure stepping out had Julia's footsteps faltering. She shivered, dark wings trembling on the fringe of memory.

You know what they told you about memories: they can't hurt you, they're spent energy. Don't let them drain you of all your tomorrows.

Sweet Jesus, they came out with a load of crap.

Look away.

She hunched narrow shoulders and scuffed across wet shingle to her favourite platform of rocks.

Clambering up, she hunkered down, staring into crystal-clear pools. Entranced by scuttling, darting life, forgetting the figure, forgetting the dark wings.

Until a voice sliced into the restful seashore sounds like a knife into flesh. "I don't believe it. Jules? Is that you?"

Inky-dark wings came thrashing and beating like trapped birds.

Think of that trick they taught you: Imagine yourself a rag doll, all loose limbs, no tension, facial muscles relaxed.

Steadily, she looked down over her shoulder. "Tamsin."

The woman's wide smile wavered when it wasn't returned. "Jules, it is you ... so are you coming down from that rock, or is there something more interesting up there?"

"Gobies and crabs. You decide."

"Haven't lost that dry sense of humour, I see."

Julia rose slowly, facing seaward for a moment before spinning round and dropping lightly onto the shingle.

Tamsin looked her up and down. "But where have you gone, my darling? Have you been ill?"

"I'm recovering."

"From what?"

You always were a nosey cow.

"Oh, just a gender nonconforming disorder. I get days when I wake up and think shall I be a boy or girl or a fucking cabbage."

Tamsin's jaw dropped before she laughed awkwardly.

"What brings you here, Tamsin?"

Is Oliver with you?

"I'm checking out an artist I might commission to paint Ollie for his next birthday, actually."

May 15th. He'll be twenty-seven.

Tamsin gave a sulky sigh. "But wouldn't you know it, I arrived at the artist's studio early and he wasn't there, so the taxi driver recommended this as a beauty spot. Hmm, so not. Odd perception of beauty some people have. Anyway, here I am killing time. Nightmare train journey down. The heating wasn't working, the toilets were blocked and contrary to accepted Darwinian theory, Neanderthal man still roams the earth. One of them checked my ticket."

Envy burning. That oh-so-clever, waspish sense of humour so loved by Oliver.

Unbidden, his warm, smiling voice filled her head. "Lighten up, Jules. See the funny side of things, like Tamsin."

Will you tell her about us?

"What's there to tell?"

Did we mean so little?

"Jules ... where were you? I said - so what brings you to this godforsaken place?"

"Beats the shit out of London any day. At least you can cross the road round here without risking life and limb."

"True, only two kinds of pedestrians back home: the quick and the dead. So do you actually live here?"

"Almost five years."

Tamsin's smooth brow knitted. "Then the last time we saw you must have been just before me and Ollie got married."

Five years and two months.

An aching world of memory and loss. Julia dipped her head so her mousy hair swung like concealing curtains around her pinched features.

Don't let her get to you.

Saving her, an inspired thought. Julia raised her head slowly, eyes narrowing. "D'you still live in the old cottage near the heath? I used to love the wisteria growing round the back and the spring blossom in the orchard."

"Believe me, all the moons will align before I get Ollie out of that place. Can't drag him away. Family roots and all that, but ... I didn't know you knew the cottage."

"Before your time."

Does Oliver still go barefoot down the creaking staircase in the morning and into the garden to feel the dew between his toes? Does he still let the dogs sleep on the bed? Does he still like to play the cello after making love?

Another thought – this one so brilliant, Julia felt dizzy with it. She imagined the depths of her eyes glittering like ice as she pointed to the top of the soaring granite cliffs. "See that? It's called Witches Leap, our best tourist attraction. You can't get how mind-blowing it is til you're up there. Come up, yeah? I guarantee you'll be impressed."

Tamsin sighed and looked at her watch. "Tempting, but I think I'll wander back up and see if my artist's arrived."

"What time did you arrange?"

"One."

Julia checked her own watch. "Another forty minutes then. Loadsa time. We can be up and back in twenty easy if we hurry. Come on, those flat boots you're wearing are made for it."

She began walking backwards up the deserted beach, calling in a singsong voice, "You'll be sorry if you miss it."

Tamsin's full, crimsoned mouth stretched in a bored yawn. "Oh, what the hell. Better than hanging round here, I suppose." Julia turned and marched off up the beach with a triumphant smile, savouring how mundane days could unexpectedly become so full of promise.

Just you follow your badass friend and see what she's got for you, bitch.

Tamsin caught up easily with her long, elegant stride. "This reminds me of dashing to orchestra practice. Remember? How old Jeremiah's lectures always ran over and made us late?"

"How could I forget?"

.. herself, overweight, struggling to keep up, clutching her precious viola in its case; Tamsin with her flute, slender legs moving effortlessly, sharing a joke with Oliver, calling back to Julia to hurry up in that rich bitch, county accent. And Oliver, his cello hoisted over his broad back like a sack of coals, laughing adoringly down at Tamsin.

Why did you stop loving me, Oliver?

Oliver, cupping her moon face in his long-fingered hands, telling her she was too intense, too obsessive. He needed someone to laugh with, someone like Tamsin. But he was deeply sorry for the bad timing. Was it his fault her assured brilliant first crashed to a devastating third?

You were my life. Then had come the shining marriage, and Julia had fled to this place removed from the world.

She climbed at a faster pace now, savouring Tamsin's breathless protest, "Hey, is this a route march?"

A lamenting herring gull wheeled overhead and floated in to alight on a wind-blasted hawthorn. It eyed the two women boldly before rising away on a mournful cry that seemed to herald in low-bellied clouds massing on the horizon, slate-coloured and moving swiftly in the rising wind.

Tamsin stared warily over the giddy drop to the rocky bay where waves tossed leaden-grey and white-tipped.

"D'you think we should go back, Jules? A storm's coming."

"Come on, we're nearly there. What are you made of? Sugar? You townies."

Tamsin gave a spirited laugh. "Us townies can show you hicks a thing or two." She

put on a determined spurt and pulled alongside Julia. "This is exhilarating."

Julia stole a sideways glance. The wind had stung bright colour into Tamsin's flawless, ivory skin and lifted her hair into an ebony halo, accentuating her luminous beauty.

Pure, clean hate. Like ice on steel.

"Do you still play the viola, Jules?"

"Now and then." When the voices in my head go away.

Like the throwing of a switch, the watery sun cut off abruptly and heavy raindrops spattered down.

Julia could remember climbing this same way in similar weather almost five years ago. Just as she'd swayed on the edge of Witches Leap, there had come the thud of running feet and strong arms dragging her away as she screamed against being saved.

After that, a sweet, dark, painless void. Sedated emergence into a twilight world where unfamiliar voices whispered out of dim shadows, coaxing her gently back into the light.

"There it is - Witches Leap." Julia pointed eagerly as she and Tamsin rounded a jutting curve. Before them the immense blowhole yawned like a hungry mouth.

Tamsin hung back. "But it's not fenced off. Doesn't anything fall down it?"

"The odd cow or sheep. They wash up down the coast eventually, minus some limbs."

"Why Witches Leap?"

"They say witches used to be cast down there. Superstition has it their ghosts still haunt the cliff top."

Julia approached the uneven rim. Looking back, she saw Tamsin hesitating. Stretching out her hand, Julia smiled encouragement. "Come and see how the sea swirls into the bottom. It really is magnificent."

Tamsin edged forward. Stood close together, the two of them could have passed for good friends as they stared into the depths at the churning inrush of water and jagged rocks revealed on its sucking retreat.

It's time.

"Look at me."

Like an animal reacting to gunfire, Tamsin's head jerked around at the change in Julia's voice. Alarm drained her face pale and she stumbled backwards.

"Why did you take him from me?"

"Jules, don't look at me like that. You're scaring me. Take who?

"Oliver. Who d'you think I mean?"

"Ollie?"

"He was MINE."

"Don't be absurd." Tamsin began digging around in her bag with jerky movements. "Christ, where's my damn phone."

"Does Oliver still go barefoot into the garden in the morning? Does he still let the dogs sleep on the bed? Does he still play his cello after he's made love? Oh no, don't go."

Julia's hand shot out, trapping Tamsin's wrist in a steely grip, sending the phone flying into Witches Leap. Descending from the cliff top in rain softened to a light drizzle, Julia stopped to gaze at her favourite platform of rocks shining like polished pewter. Fast-scudding clouds were casting racing shadows over the empty beach and she ran with them until she was breathless.

When she'd got her breath back, she began humming the laughing, dancing notes of one of her favourite viola pieces. For a moment, she followed the flight of a redshank as it gave its loud, yelping cry and dipped towards the long rolls of tumbling surf.

She felt cleansed, purified. Everything had tied up neatly. She liked that.

They would be looking for her by now. In fact, there was one of them, his ungainly gait accelerating as he spotted her.

They were becoming more lax now, as each of her outings proved uneventful; routine now - the mild ticking off when she got back, half-hearted enquiries into her innocent diversions.

I found some gobies and crabs and watched a redshank, she'd say, and they would smile patronisingly at her delight in the simple pleasures of life.

She could add, "Oh, and I bumped into an old friend." But she didn't think so.

She wandered up the beach towards her eager pursuer, already planning her next outing. Her first stop would be that nice shop in the village that sold a bit of everything. There she would linger over condolence cards, choosing one with words tastefully sympathetic to send to the old cottage on the heath. When the time was right.

It would be so good to begin, Dearest Oliver ...

Sandra's love of writing has seen many of her stories and serials appear in women's magazines and anthologies over the years. Otherwise, some modest but nonetheless always thrilling competition wins. Rejections – too many! She lives between Bristol and Bath in the Southwest of England.

PENNY

By Emma Burnett

There is this penny that I have. It has been touched, rubbed so often that the face is worn off. You wouldn't know that it was a 1943 copper Lincoln Head penny, but I know because my gramps told me when he gave it to me. He knew because he took it off his friend, who found it when they were moving furniture for an old woman in Queens. She had jars of coins, saved pennies from when she was a girl. Told them not to touch any of the money while they were moving the furniture. Told them those coins brought her luck since she was a kid.

My gramps, he took that penny, and all the rest of the coins, left the furniture where it stood. No one ever came after him.

He thought about selling it, when he found it in the jars, of retiring down to Florida, moving out to California, finding some chipper blonde or smoky brunette to keep him company. Decided he'd stick with the grouchy dames in New York and his good luck.

He used all the rest of the coins. But he kept that penny it in his pocket, that rare 1943 copper coin, rubbed it for luck, robbed banks for cash. Told me it musta worked, because here he was on his deathbed at 93 and here's his penny, just rub it when I need luck.

He died that night. The police told me later it took four hours and three cleaners to scrub all the blood off the walls. They guessed his luck had run out, they hadn't known he had such important enemies. They told me I should probably be careful. I rubbed my penny.

I rubbed my penny before I walked into the Waldorf Astoria for a job interview. I had no training, I had lied on my resume. They hired me to work in the kitchens, told me I seemed like a nice young man who would work hard and make the hotel proud. I nodded and touched the penny in my pocket.

I rubbed that penny before they handcuffed me and put me in the back of the police van. I rubbed it again when they booked me in, told me to empty my pockets. I knew I wouldn't be in there long. That penny loved to be pet. It would find its way back into my pocket.

"Your grandfather would have been proud," said my mother as she bailed me out. She didn't sound pleased about it.

"They got nothing on me," I said.

"That's what he always said," grumbled my mother. "Look where it got him."

I shrugged. "He only got dead when he'd lost his penny. And he'd had plenty of time with it. Someone else's turn."

The jobs I got kept me moving around the tri-state area. The jobs always ended in people in suits, mostly men, needing to be packed into bags. Sometimes they got packed with extra bricks to help them sink. I didn't question the hits, and I always made sure my penny was with me.

I started to think about retirement myself. Somewhere warm, away from the bustle and the noise. And away from my mother. Somewhere I could crack on with creating a kid to pass my penny on to, later.

My mother laughed at this. "You want to have a kid?" she asked. She laughed at me and slapped another grilled cheese sandwich on my plate. She thinks they're healthy because the cheese has calcium.

"I want someone to pass my important stuff on to."

"What important stuff you got? A dishonourable discharge letter from your good-for-nothing father? A bomber jacket your grandfather stole? What you gonna pass on to a kid?" My mother stared at me hard. "What you got that's so important?"

I didn't tell her about my penny. If she didn't know, then I wasn't going to say. "Just some lucky stuff."

"That's not a good reason to have a kid. You got no legacy, you just got crap piled up in your room in my apartment. You got crap jobs. Quit moving around and settle down, get a steady job, find a nice girl. Maybe some woman would pop out kids for you, if you settle down."

I didn't tell her about the cash in the bank, the house in Jersey, the cars in the basement, the heated pool. I went out there to relax after jobs, waved at the neighbours, paid other people to clean and take out the trash. I hung pictures of rare coins on the wall. I rubbed my penny, made sure it was safe on the side of the pool when I went for a swim.

I took jobs in Ohio and Kentucky. I wondered why anyone important would go to Kentucky, and felt bad that they'd never leave it. It took me five hours to drive through cornfields that felt like forever. I thought I might never leave, either. I stopped in a bar in Virginia on my way back, pretended to be a war vet, rubbed my penny and got a free beer. Met a nice lady.

The nice lady turned out to be from Jersey and I started going to my house more often, taking her out for expensive meals. My mother got nosy, asked "where you going all the time? You got a job, you got an apartment?" I finally took her to my house, told her a got a job in security.

"Surprised you can afford this," she said.

"I'm a man of mystery," I told her.

"You're a man, anyway," she said. "When can you get your crap outta my apartment?"

I introduced her to Laura and stayed out of their way while they did whatever women do to be the top cat or lead dog. I rubbed my penny and hoped I wouldn't get caught up in it. I took another job and got out of the way for two weeks.

Laura moved into my house. She was nice. She smelled good and she didn't ask questions about my work. She did the cleaning and cooking, she did the laundry and took the trash out. She waved at the neighbours. We swam in the pool and we ate good food and I always rubbed my penny before my mother came over at the weekend. Laura stopped asking me why I kept my hand in my pocket so much. She was good like that.

She told me she was pregnant when I got back from a job in Pennsylvania. I was getting changed out of my dark clothes, the ones that hide the mud and the blood, and I dropped my stuff on the floor. I hugged her tight, then apologised for getting her dirty. She said it was ok, and I should get into the shower and rinse off. She said she'd put on a load of laundry and join me in a minute.

That's when she took my penny.

She told me, later, when I was in prison, that she'd swapped it for another coin, that she'd been sneaking out of bed for weeks to look at it, take photos of it. That she got someone to make a fake, and that she wasn't pregnant anyway. That she and my mother were going to share the penny and my house and my money, because it should have been hers anyway, my mother's. My grandfather had no right to miss out his daughter just because she was a woman. That he should have respected her, given her what she deserved. That I had skipped the line. She told me that she loved my mother and had given her the coin to keep safe. She said my mother promised to pass it on to her later. That my mother respected her.

My mother told me that she and Laura had planned the whole thing, months ago, years maybe. That Laura wasn't pregnant, which was good because she'd hate to have to get rid of a pregnant woman, and where did I think I got my skills from anyway? "But thanks for the lucky coin, did you say it was from 1943? Well, that's funny, because that's when Gramps was born. He killed his mother on his way out, and it's funny how that stuff works, ain't it. In roundabout ways. He killed his mother, she killed her father. Maybe she'd come see her son go, too. That it was stupid to get caught in Kentucky where they still got the death penalty."

"And whose gonna believe you didn't do all them things? All them bloody clothes in the back of your car. You shouldn't have kept souvenirs."

"Anyway," she said, "I gotta go, I got things to do. Good luck in here."

She rubbed the penny and smiled.

Emma Burnett is an Oxford-based doctoral researcher and writer. She spends her free time doing sport, hanging out with cats, and reading immense amounts of sci-fi & fantasy. What is sleep even?

LUNATIC'S WOOD

By Atlas Weyland Eden

England, 1780

Sometimes she whispers to me, when the hours fall quiet. She tells me of the veins of leaves like spiderweb-tapestries, crisscrossing betwixt the stars. She can be cruel like that, with her poems.

"You've never seen a leaf, my love," I tell her. "We've been in these cages all our years." At which point she gets huffy and says naught for a while.

I sit and listen to the stones. I look to the blank wall and think, Window, but it is a leftover word, stuck in my head from another life. What does it mean?

In the morning — at least when it feels slightly more morning than night — they lead me out of my room, to where the others sway and sniffle. I sit on a chair and the doctor raises his knife; they fret and squirrel away, but I do not move. I watch with practised boredom as he cuts along my arm and my blood drips into the bucket. Wafts of ancient metal.

When enough is taken, they bind the wound in rags, and the rags slowly redden. The doctor picks up the bucket and studies it, as if admiring his red reflection, and they lead me back to my room. I nurse my arm, alone with her, as she chirps softly, earlier grievances forgot. The first time they cut me, I screamed. I raged. Perhaps I hurt someone. They bound my arms to my chest, pushed me into a desolate hole, and I sat alone — truly alone. They say the problems in my mind stem from my veins. I have too much bad blood. Or perhaps it is to keep me weak, so I don't get out of hand.

I have been in the asylum only a little less time than the walls and the roof. I have seen many folk arrive, seen them falter and cease to blink. I have seen the keepers and the would-be doctors change faces time and again. My name was written on a piece of paper, but I lost the paper and now

I have no name. All I know is that I am a lunatic among lunatics in a lunatic asylum.

Once there was a scholar. I knew him so well I could list every nick and scar on his hands. He said that 'lunatic' came from the word for moon: we are simply moon-folk who have found ourselves on the wrong celestial sphere. He was clever like that.

I went with him everywhere. I was his shadow, clinging to his soles. But in time, his reasoning descended into uncouth gibbering, and they took him and bound him in stone and called him mad, even while he murmured about the sound of the stars. The scholar died a long time ago.

Only a lunatic remains, trapped in his body, staring at his hands. I've forgotten many things I used to know. The scholar wrote his name on a piece of paper, but I lost the paper and now I have no name. Denied my reason, I relished in madness. I howled, swooned, growled at any who came close, spat out medicine and wept upon the walls. It was a life of storms, with no dawn in sight. Then one

day the green-eyed keeper, who is kinder than the rest, gave me my own room. And in the corner was a cage, and in the cage she sat waiting, with her smudge of gold feathers and her delicate beak.

"A gift," said the green-eyed keeper. "It's your canary now."

She was like something imagined, come down from the sky to keep me company in my cage.

I reached out a finger, and she hopped forward and nipped me gently. A smile spread across face.

"What will you call it?" asked the keeper.

The canary perked up her head, and in that dank, sunless chamber, she sang the sweetest enchantment ever to grace mortal ears. 'Calypso,' I said. She pondered a moment. Then in a voice of melodies, she said, *Calypso? Yes. That sounds right.*

I sit now, huddled against the wall by her cage, offering a handful of seeds which they give to me to give to her. She accepts them daintily through the bars — they do not trust me with the key. With a yawn, she ruffles herself down to sleep. I put my head against stone and close my eyes.

The dreams come unbidden, dancing. Dreams of leaves and roots and unseen things. I awake with tears staining my face. Gritting my teeth, I curse myself. In an asylum, a lack of imagination is a blessing. The barren halls grow worse when one imagines all the things that are not there.

I turn to check if she is awake, and gaze at the bottom of the cage. A seed. Below her perch, a tiny black speck, mixed in with the whitish waste. I poke my fingers through and pick it up. I don't remember feeding her this. Has she been supping on mysterious fruits while I sleep?

Calypso gives no answer, merely turns her head and suggests I rest. Biting my tongue, I place the seed in a crack in the wall. Then I tuck my head under my arm and close my eyes.

The following week, six people die. I hear it: a silence in the ceiling. I see it in the doctor's drawn face, in the eyes of those left alive, rattling their chains in mourning.

The theatre of the asylum has a small cast. Twelve or so patients, less than a dozen keepers. I hear whispers of a disease creeping in from the perilous world beyond. With a wave of Death's hoary hand, our population is halved, while the rest, lunatics and learned men alike, shiver as if it were winter.

The whispers change. Not a disease of the body, but a disease of the mind. A man strangles himself in the dead of night. This is not all that odd, until I learn it is the doctor, in his clean white robe, lying red-faced on the floor. The keepers devise a theory. Insanity is contagious, the infection is spreading. Most of the staff pack their things and are gone within the week, leaving three keepers to tame the lunatics, lest we claw each other to pieces or tear off our clothes and dance beneath the moon.

I no longer have my blood drained. All treatments were strangled with the good doctor. I feel no more insane than usual. On the rare times I leave my room, the other lunatics wring their hands and bow their heads. I am the eldest. The asylum incarnate, scarred and grey-eyed, hair like matted chains.

Something grows from the crack in my wall. A shoot uncurls itself, tender, pale. On what does it feed, with no rain and no sun? An illogical thing. But I suppose this place wasn't built for logic. I give it what little water I have, and I talk to it, and Calypso sings, and perhaps the two of us imitate a fair spring breeze.

Food is little. They give me a crust from another man's meal. "It's bad times, out there," says the green-eyed keeper. He does not elaborate. Perhaps war wages in the outside world. Or famine.

Or plague. The distant places are ever on the verge of collapse, but nothing can breach these walls.

I no longer leave my room. I tend the growing shoot. Nights go by, but no one comes. No food, no water, no seeds. I worry for my shoot, for my canary. Have they forgotten me?

At last, someone bangs upon the door.

"Water!" I cry. A key clinks, and then footsteps fade. I wait — nothing happens. I approach the door. Bewilderingly, it is open. On the floor is a plate of stale bread, a half-filled jug of water. I pour some on the shoot, soak the bread to give to Calypso, then drain the last drops and content myself

with crumbs. When all are fed, I step out my room. The asylum is empty. No screams, cursing or wandering feet. I pace the halls, at a loss. The few keepers that remained have gone. The patients have died, disappeared, or fled.

Fled?

I find a door ajar. Hastily I push it closed, lest the outside leak in. I return to my room. Alone with my treasures, I realise I am no longer a lunatic. I am *the* lunatic.

The shoot grows. It winds up the wall, spreading branches into slender fingers, creeping over the ceiling. It sends down white trunks, rooting into the floor. The work of years occurring in days.

Perhaps time's flow is changing, or my madness worsening without treatment. Small, orange-red fruit grow. I pluck one. Poisonous? Madness-curing? Both? I bite down: the flesh is bitter and sugary. When I do not die, I give one to Calypso. I split open another, peer at the little black seeds.

Calypso asks, *Do you remember what the scholar said?*

"You never knew the scholar. He's gone. Long gone." Still, I frown and think. "He said many things. Rambled on for nights on end about all manner of lunacies."

What did he say about trees?

"Trees? He knew their names. He liked names." I squint at the fruits, at the twisting trunks.

'*Ficus benjamina*, strangler fig. Indian. Plants itself onto a host. For wont of trees, it can root onto buildings. They say one seed can turn a temple into a forest.'

Is this a temple? she wonders. *There are no gods.*

"There's you," I say, and earn a flattered chirrup. I pick out a handful of seeds, leave my room and scatter them about the asylum. They take root as if the entire place were strewn with soil.

In their search for the sky, the branches gouge a hole in the roof. I blink, blinded by a shaft of light.

Beside me, she flutters and sings.

"What witchcraft is this?" I say.

Sunlight, she whispers.

"Sunlight?"

Sunlight.

I shut my eyes and shuffle away. Lying there, brushed by a breeze from above.

The harsh light softens and cools — I know what it is before I open my eyes. My whole self shakes. Oh, there never was a poem that did justice to the moon, shining in a quiet night. "Look, love. Look."

I'm looking, says she.

The moonlight calls them. They come wafting: seeds, gardens, Edens. Streaming through the hole, seeds of things I'd forgotten I knew. They take root in the fabric of the place. I poke my head from my den and wander, sitting at times in silence, as I watch the asylum become something else.

Trees. They spring from the tiniest cracks in the floor, surge upwards and blanket the ceiling.

So much painful slowness rushing past so fast I can scarcely take it in. I reach out, touch ridged grey bark. Oak. A choke in the back of the throat. I touch a smooth, mossy, stone-like surface.

Beech. Ivy spirals overhead, scouring the trunks with green; mistletoe drips from the canopy; lichens curl and writhe; ferns unfurl their faces.

From the branch-broken ceiling, stars and rain pour through, and I stand with open mouth, gulping. She hops and trills. Head up-raised, I see them — truly see them — for the first time.

Leaves. An abundance, a miracle of greens, some so green they are somehow gold, each leaf stencilled with a hundred patterns, each branch holding uncountable leaves, each tree holding boggling branches, each one but a speck in the wood which overcomes my asylum.

I faint.

Awaken. Too much. Too much magic for one madman. I lay my head on the floor, rest my eyes.

Why? Why must I torment myself, when doubtless I lie in my unadorned home, drained of blood, the moon but a fantasy, leaves but a fiction, while lunatics pace and mumble outside?

I open my eyes.

Sleep well? says Calypso. Fruit falls on my face. The moon raises an eyebrow. The woodland that has sprung up inside these walls is there, waiting, as if it had stood for a thousand years, and I but a spectre wandering the bracken.

I pull a twig from the fig, poke it into the lock of her cage. She perks up. The twig snaps, and I grab another, rustle around in the lock, biting my lip, wishing I was one of those former-thieves who faked madness to avoid imprisonment. Inside, she hops up and down, singing. Her tail flutters.

A click. The cage door whines open. She falls still, sitting there, uncertain. Then she flits onto the ground, onto my hand. Gazes into my eyes.

"My love," I say.

Calypso ruffles herself, feathers aglow. With a flicker of her wings, she is in the air, wavering.

A triumphant chirrup. I grin. Then, like a candle being snuffed by a breeze, she flies up through the hole — and is gone.

I stand there a moment, waiting. Staring at constellations I once could name. Waiting. The silence sinks in. I fall to my knees, choking.

It's all caving in again. The walls failing. The colours sickening. I hear the rattle of scholar's bones, taste bile on my tongue.

"Calypso!" I call, and the word turns into a scream.

Where is she? Where did she go? Why did I let her go? Will she come back? Is she dead? Am I dead? Where is the scholar? Why are the trees staring? Calypso?

A realisation. I came here to seek asylum from the moon and her visions. And now my love has left me, the moon has me, and I am mad.

The trees are old and tangled. A fox digs his den in the doctor's old room. A boar roots in the cellar. Spiders spin patterns, flowers become butterflies. The floor is anemones and moss. No birds.

That's the strangest thing. The hum of gnats, the poems of

bats, but no matter how I strain my ears, no birdsong.

I sit in the grove which I am fairly sure used to be my room. The shoot that sprouted from the wall now holds up the sky, trunks like pillars, each the width of the widest tree. The ground is scattered with its unearthly fruits. Phantoms dance before my eyes.

People visit sometimes, treading lightly, as one does in church. They come to drag me away, to force me back into the light. I throw sticks at them. Stones. They don't linger.

Do not disturb the lunatic of Lunatic's Wood. He is raving, and does not trust the uncouth creatures that come from *out there*.

I have lain by the fig so long I no longer know what is leg and what is root. I look at the slit of sky betwixt the million, million leaves. All of them, all of this, came from her seed — from Calypso. And now, without her, all I have are ghosts.

What is there to do, here in the wreckage of myself? Do I lie for another thousand years until I am soil and worms? Or do I brave the bitter, reeling, waking, clear-skied world — and look for my love? The world will break me.

But then again, I suppose I'm already broken.

I raise myself, wavering. Coughing, blinking. As I survey my kingdom, I hear a trilling. A high piping above my head. Birdsong after nightfall? The world really has lost its wits. I shake it away — no time for fantasies. What was I thinking?

But the sound comes again. The song sinks in, and I stand utterly still. My breath falters. I raise my eyes. Shaking, I extend a hand.

From the fathomless canopy, Calypso flies down in a brush of gold and alights on my wrist.

Tears burn down my face. I hold her close to my cheek.

"My love," I say.

My lunatic, says she.

Atlas Weyland Eden is sixteen years old and lives on the edge of Dartmoor, Devon. He chose to be a writer when he was nine. He loves stories of nature and myth. Various writing prizes have published his work, including the Young Walter Scott Prize and the Lewis Carroll Society.

LIME TREE ARBOUR

By Denarii Peters

My fingers slipped on the padlock key. My hands were shaking. I couldn't believe I was doing this. I had never done anything illegal before, never had so much as a parking ticket, yet here I was breaking into this lock-up. I wasn't sure it even belonged to the man I was planning to bury in the lime tree arbour. If it did, all I had to do was remove a package from the glove compartment of the car inside and I would be eight thousand pounds better off.

The money, if it was there at all, was the proceeds of a robbery gone wrong. My uncle George and his two mates, Chris and Eric, stole it from a swanky jewellers in town. The manager interrupted them as they were taking the contents out of the safe. Startled, George shot him as the three robbers fled. At least they remembered to take the money and the jewels with them.

Before he died, the manager gave the police a pretty good description of George. He wasn't hard to recognise anyway, what with his scarred face and his crooked smile.

When they tracked him down he was stupid. He ought to have raised his arms but he didn't. They thought he was reaching for a gun so they shot him. It turned out later he had been unarmed.

I didn't attend the funeral. He had been from the wrong side of the family. He had spent more time in prison than out. I wasn't even supposed to know anything about him but years ago I had found the stash of letters my mother kept hidden. George wanted someone to boast to and his sister was the one he had chosen, little Julia, good, straight-as-they-come Julia. She had no idea I had read every one of his words, shivering with delight and awe at George's descriptions of the terrible crimes he claimed to have committed.

It was only natural my mother would be upset by her brother's death but she was far too respectable to want to be seen mourning him. My father was relieved she did not go to the funeral. I think I was the only one who shed any tears. My secret hero was gone. There would be no more exciting instalments in the long running saga of Uncle George and his band of robbers.

I decided I would sneak out to the place where he had been buried. I couldn't figure out how to go about stealing a wreath so instead I took some of our neighbour's prize winning roses and my mother's favourite painted porcelain vase.

*

The graveyard was empty, no visitors on that cold, dank afternoon. I wasn't sure where, amongst the many tumbled and handful of upright stones, I would find George's grave. I looked around for signs of earth turned over in recent days. I doubted he would have much of a headstone.

"You looking for me, Lucy?"

The voice made me jump. I turned. My Uncle George was sitting on the low wall surrounding a line of dustbins. I recognised him from the single photograph my mother had kept. He looked no older than he had in that image, which must have been taken twenty years earlier.

"Uncle George!" I was delighted. The stupid police must have got it wrong, though I did wonder who they had shot and buried in place of my relative.

He nodded at the flowers. "Those are nice. Shall we put them on my grave? I didn't get many, you know, and not one single rose, not even from Jools."

"I suppose we might." I had to do something with the wilting blooms. I couldn't take them back, could I?

He led me to a shady corner some distance from the chapel.

I peered down at an insignificant mound of damp, grey clay. "Who's really in there?"

"What do you mean?"

"I mean, who did they bury instead of you?"

He jerked back and stared at me. "You think I'm still alive, do you? Ah, you haven't realised..." He laughed.

"Stop it, Uncle George. I'm not a child. I don't believe in ghosts."

"Your choice, I guess, but I'm not going to walk through a wall to prove you're wrong. I'm going to do something much more useful." He leaned over me. "You see, I hid the diamonds. If I tell you where they are, you can see Chris and Eric get their shares, can't you? My cut of the money is no use to me now but you..." He cocked his head to one side. "I'm sure you could make good use of it."

He had me there. With enough money, I could chuck up my boring job and leave this God forsaken town behind me... and my parents wouldn't be able to tell me what to do any more. All right, he could pretend to be a ghost if he liked. He wasn't fooling me. "Why not? You tell me where to find the loot and I'll go and fetch it."

"Not so fast, my dear. There is one other thing." He waved his arm over the mound. "I don't like it here. I want you to move me."

A shiver passed through me. My legs came close to giving way. I could see the flowers I had placed beside the hump of earth but I saw them through the faint outline of Uncle George's hand, his fingers now as insubstantial as the air. I think I may have passed out for a second or two.

George was leaning over me again. He was muttering something about, "...nervous women. Should have picked a feller."

"No! No, you shouldn't. I'll get the jewels."

"OK and you'll move me to the lime tree arbour?"

"If that's what you want."

"Good girl. Now, you'll need money and some transport."

For a second I thought he meant I was to borrow the family car. I experienced a sudden vision of me trying to explain to my father how the boot came to be full of mud.

"Pay attention, Lucy. All you have to do is find out what the police did with the keys I had in my pocket when they shot me. I've been renting a lock-up, you see."

I was sure he already knew my mother, as his nearest relative, had been given everything the police had found in his possession. She had bundled it all together and thrown it into a box at the back of the garage. She said it would have been disrespectful to get rid of it so soon after George had passed away. My father disagreed.

George told me where the lock-up was and sent me on my way. By the time I was half way home I had almost managed to convince myself I had only imagined meeting him. Almost but not quite.

****

I found the keys among George's effects. They were in the pocket of his overcoat, the one with the rust coloured stain high on the left side next to the top button. There were six keys in all. Two I knew belonged to the flat he had rented. The landlady had opted to change the locks rather than have them back. She had said she wanted no reminders of that rogue.

One, I was surprised to realise, was a spare belonging to my family's house. Had George visited when we were out? If he had, I was certain my father could not have known. Two of the other three looked like they belonged to padlocks, while the final one was quite small. I guessed that one maybe fitted a suitcase.

I stuffed everything except the keys back into the box. It was already getting late. I would have to leave finding the lock-up until the next morning.

****

The building was a surprise. I expected a tumbledown lean-to packed with cardboard boxes full of dubious electrical goods and similar items of plunder. It turned out I had been watching too many police dramas. It was one of a set of modern, brick built garages with a cream coloured up-and-over door. I turned the key in the lock, pushed at the panel and went inside. There was a light switch on the wall to my right. I tried it. It worked. I reminded myself, Uncle George had been dead for less than a month.

Most of the space was taken up by a car. It was an old, red, nineteen-sixties mini, which wouldn't have been out of place in The Italian Job, except the paintwork on this one was scratched all over. I tried the driver's door and it was was unlocked. There was a key on the seat. I picked it up, got in and used it to open the glove compartment. Inside was a wrapped package.

A few minutes of counting later I discovered I was now the

undisputed owner of just over eight thousand pounds, more money than I had ever seen in my entire life.

A thought crossed my mind. What if I didn't go back to the churchyard? What could dear, dead George do to me if I took this cash and decided not to honour his request?

Ah but... simple greed consumed me. Eight thousand was a drop in the ocean when compared to the value of what he had stolen in the jewellery heist. Eight thousand wouldn't buy me a place of my own. It wasn't even enough to let me quit my job.

The next day I rang in sick and returned to George's grave.

****

Following George's instructions, I made contact with Chris. I told him nothing about ghosts and never even hinted I might know where the jewels had been hidden. All I did was pay him the five hundred pounds he demanded for helping me move my uncle to the arbour.

After we had reburied the body and Chris had left, George reappeared. He told me to start digging beneath another of the lime trees then vanished again. I soon discovered a rucksack about two feet down stuffed with rings, bracelets and a lot of loose stones.

It was at that point it dawned on me I had no idea how to turn this glittering cascade into hard cash. I wondered if I could just turn up at a pawnbrokers. There was one I knew of in the town. "We buy your gold," it proclaimed on a huge banner above the window... but once again I had seen enough police dramas to be aware most of the local pawnbrokers would be on the lookout for gems as hot as these. I walked over to George's new resting place and sat on the damp grass.

After a while I sensed someone watching me. I wasn't surprised. He was perched on a bench at the centre of the arbour. "You didn't listen, Lucy. I said you could have my share, not all of the loot. You'll need Chris's help again. Go and tell him I sent you a letter with instructions on what to do if anything happened to me."

****

Chris was drinking tea in the same cafe where I had found him the first time. I showed him the rucksack and he recognised it at once.

"How did you get hold of this?"

I don't think he was at all convinced by my tale about a posthumous letter. I knew as soon as I handed the bag over he intended to cheat me but what could I do about it?

I headed straight back to George. He wasn't surprised either but said he had to give Chris at least a chance but now Chris had blown it.

"You'll have to kill him, pet."

"What? Don't be ridiculous. I can't do that."

"Why not? It's not as hard as you think. I know where he'll go with the jewels and that fence is a shifty bugger. Chris getting shot on his premises won't raise an eyebrow. You can bring the gems back here, oh and why don't I just..." He vanished again.

I sat on the bench wishing I had never got involved.

Overnight I replayed everything in my head. How dare Chris behave like this to me? I had as much right to George's share as he had, more in fact, since George himself had told me I could have it.

The next morning I went back to the arbour. I had decided I would have to tell George there was nothing I could do, even though I would have liked to teach Chris a lesson. I didn't have a clue how to get hold of a gun, let alone how to use one.

George pulled a face. "Use your imagination, girl. What do you think I did with the gun that killed the manager? That's the one we'll use on Chris."

I told myself it was all nonsense. If I had a gun, I was sure all I would need to do was threaten Chris and he would see sense and give me George's share.

The weapon was in the last place anyone would have thought to look. George had used his key to enter my parents' house while they were out and had hidden the weapon under the floorboards of my bedroom. Long before I was born, he said, the room had been his. When he was seventeen he had cut the hole out and re-covered it. It became the place where he hid his first stashes. Somehow this new connection made us closer than before. He was right when he said recovering the weapon posed no risk to me at all. Anyway, I had no intention of using it. After I had sorted Chris out, I would bury the gun beside my uncle.

****

After a week George told me the time was right. Chris had made contact with the fence and that evening they were going to agree a price for the jewels.

The night was cold and dark, no moon and, since the recent cuts, only one in three street lights were switched on. It was simple enough for me to avoid the scattered pools of pale light. By now I knew they didn't matter at all to George. As far as I could tell, no-one else could see or hear him.

The gun poked me in the side through the pocket of the ample coat he had instructed me to buy. These days he often came with me when I left the lime grove as he was no longer held in place by the constraints of sacred ground, since there was nothing holy at all about the arbour.

He passed right through the door of the fence's dwelling and was back in seconds. "No problem. They're in the far room having a drink before getting down to business."

"I'm not going to hurt anyone."

"Of course you're not. Now, come on. Do like I showed you."

His lock picks were already in my hand. He had trained me,

not the easiest of tasks when he could not demonstrate, but I listened to his instructions, practised on every door I could find. He was pleased with my progress, said I was a natural just like he used to be. The levers shifted and there was the softest of clicks. An owl seeking its prey would have made more sound.

Into the hallway... and a light showed under a door to my right. Two voices, laughter, the clink of metal on wood...

"You did well, even better than I was expecting. I can give you a good price for all of these."

"Yeah, everyone thought old George was the brains but he weren't."

George bristled. "I'll show them who was the brains."

He flickered and was beside me again. "Their backs are to us, Lucy. We won't get a better chance. In we go!"

He passed through at the same instant I shoved the door open. Chris and another man swung round to look at me. "Who are you?"

"She's Lucy, George's niece." Chris dropped the gems and took a step toward me. "What are you doing here?"

"Who cares what she's doing. We can't let her go now. She'll bring the police." The other man swung his fist at me.

Everything happened so fast. I didn't mean to use the gun. I didn't mean to fire at him and then at Chris. It wasn't my fault. I'm not to blame. I only did what George had taught me, one long afternoon in the lime tree arbour.

I was surprised how little I felt as I stared down on the two sprawled bodies. I scooped up the jewels from the table. They didn't quite fill the rucksack.

George was across the room from me. "Come on, Lucy. Get this open." He was leaning against a huge, old safe.

"Don't be ridiculous. We'd need a ton of explosives."

"You could always try the combination."

"How would you know that?"

He tapped his nose. "Can't you guess?"

It wasn't difficult. "You watched the fence opening it."

"I did and now it's our turn."

Inside were bundles of notes and several velvet cases. He told me not to touch anything except the money.

As we left the shop behind us, I realised I was rich. I had got away with the perfect crime. Why would anyone suspect me...

...and why stop at this? I could have a whole new career, aided and abetted by my dear, late uncle. It's true I had never met

George in the flesh but I had a feeling I was going to be spending a lot of time with him in the lime tree arbour.

Denarii Peters lives with her husband in Norfolk. A former teacher, she spends her days writing stories of all kinds, from flash fiction through short stories to full length novels, and drinking a lot of coffee. She recently achieved second place in the Henshaw Press Short Story Competition.

LEMONADE MEMORIES

by Rob Molan

I first encountered the man with the metal legs on a bitterly cold Remembrance Day in 1965 walking home from the ceremony at the war memorial where I and my Scout pack stood alongside veterans of both World Wars. There I was cap on my head, my body in a warm embrace of a duffle coat but with my knee caps feeling more like ice caps thanks to my short trousers and there he was leaning out of the window of the first floor flat opposite our house waving to me. I had not seen him since we moved in two months previously although I had seen other people coming and going through the communal door of the block.

"Son, can you do me a favour please?" he called.

He was wearing a grey flat cap and glasses, and looked very old to me. "If you come up I'll explain." I crossed the road and entered the block and climbed the stairs. I stood on the landing waiting for one of the two blue doors to be opened and after a minute or two the one on the left opened. He was a short man and greeted me with a warm smile standing in his doorway supporting himself with a Zimmer frame.

"Thanks son. I just need you to get me a bottle of lemonade. Here's an empty bottle to take back to the shop and six pence for the new one."

The Scouts had taught me the importance of doing good deeds for old people and this seemed just like the other errands which I had run for other elderly neighbours. "Yes, I'll run across to the shop for you," I replied, stepping forward to take the bottle and coin, noticing that he was wearing a medal on his blue cardigan attached to a blue, red and white ribbon like those worn by some of the men at the memorial.

Five minutes later I returned with the lemonade and knocked on his door. When it opened he invited me in and turned very slowly in his frame and slowly shuffled his way down the narrow hallway before entering his kitchen. I followed him in and saw him awkwardly lever himself into a chair.

"Put it on the table son please. What's your name?" His kindly eyes stared at me through his glasses which were a little misted and I noticed that he had white hairs coming out of his nostrils and a ruddy complexion.

"Colin, sir."

"Well, I'm Mr Thomson. The boy next door used to get my lemonade but his mum and dad moved away and I've been missing my wee treat ever since." As he spoke, I glanced down at his feet. His trousers were on the short side and had ridden up and I saw what looked like rods of metal appearing above the top of each sock. I had seen a film once in the cinema about scary robots and they had thin metallic legs but I didn't think Mr Thomson looked like a robot as he was fleshy and friendly.

"Have you always had metal legs, Mr Thomson?" I wince at the memory of throwing that question at him.

But he didn't blanche. "No, son. I was born with legs just like yours. But I was sent to a war with many of my pals, a few of whom never came back, and I was hurt in a big explosion. I was lucky to survive but when I woke up in hospital my legs had been amputated below the knee."

My reply was even more cringeworthy. "So, you still have some of your legs then?"

To his great credit, he gently laughed at this and tousled my hair. "Aye, it could have been worse so it could son. They gave me these things to get around." He pointed at his artificial legs and banged on the exposed part of one with a spoon.

"Was that the same war that the white haired men who were at the war memorial this morning fought in?"

He nodded. "Aye, the same war. One or two of those men pop round occasionally to see me but they are getting old now and it's difficult for them to get here and make it up the stairs."

Later, I said my goodbyes and went home and told my mum about Mr Thomson while she was making a cake in the kitchen. She said I did the right thing to help him. "But where does he get his food from?" I asked her.

She stopped mixing for a second before replying. "I think someone from social services must deliver food for him from the Cooperative. I remember that's how Mrs Gray in our old street got hers. But your Mr Thomson mustn't like the lemonade that they sell there and prefers the brand they sell in

Mr Hunter's shop." I liked the idea of getting a very special lemonade for my new acquaintance.

****

For the rest of that winter, I made trips to the shop for lemonade twice a week. He sat in a chair next to the window watching the world go by and so was able to spot me when passing. Invariably, I stopped for a chat after my deliveries sitting with him in his stuffy, warm sitting room. Sometimes I thought I would melt like a snowman but he wore a cardigan and never took off his cap; I thought it must have been glued to his head. He liked to pour his tea onto the saucer and sip it from there without spilling it, a feat which always impressed me.

I can't recall the detail of many of our gas fire chats but a few linger in my memory. One day I decided to ask him who the young lady was in the yellowing photograph on his sideboard, her head resting on one of her hands, hair back combed into a plait and big eyes gazing upwards.

"That's my wife Betty. I still miss her very much. We married just before the first war but she passed away during the second from cancer. She said nothing had changed when I came home after the amputations and she stuck to her word for thirty years, so she did, looked after me and took me places." I am sure that I saw a tear in his eye at this point.

"Where did you go after she died?"

"My daughter Helen took me in but her husband lost his job

and they emigrated to Australia in 1956. They did so with my blessing as they had to think about their future. The Council then gave me this flat. They said that it was the only one available at the time though I was not entirely convinced. Still, what can you do?" He shrugged his head and sighed.

Mr Thomson liked to reminisce about going here and there with his wife and daughter and shocked me when I once asked about his more recent outings.

"The last time I was out? That would be the summer of 1960 I recall when they wanted to replace some parts of my artificial legs. An ambulance came to take me to the hospital in Edinburgh and I fair enjoyed that trip as it was a sunny day and the nurses were lovely and kind at the hospital. The ambulance driver was a right character so he was, telling jokes throughout the twenty mile round journey." There was a faraway look in his eye as he recalled this. "Who knows, the hospital may want to see me again one day and I'll get another day out." He laughed bitterly.

He usually liked to know what I had been up to since my last visit. Once, I told him that I had been running with my friends in the fields surrounding the ruined castle on the edge of the town pretending to fight a battle. He beamed at me and raised his left hand.

"Now, I remember playing in those fields when I was a young lad. Kenneth Stark and I used to go up there a lot in the good weather. Kenneth was a bit naughtier than me." He started to cackle before continuing the story." One day he climbed over the wall of the big house at the edge of the field to pinch some apples. The next thing I knew was he was clambering back over shouting 'quick the man's coming' and he and I were sprinting through the heather and long grass as fast as we could to escape."

His voice trailed away at this point. "Aye, I was a good runner then. I won the hundred yards school race twice. You wouldn't guess that would you now?" His smile had gone by then.

I liked to tell Mr Thomson about my toys and he encouraged me to bring some to show him, so I sometimes brought one of my Dinky cars. He loved to push my blue Morris Minor around the dining table and in those moments he became a young boy again. When I told him about the Scalextric set which I was lucky enough to get for Christmas he was all ears.

"Are you telling me son that the wee cars race around the track on their own?" He stared with wide eyes as he asked this, his mouth falling open revealing gaps in his front teeth. I tried to explain how the electricity moved the cars round the track and I controlled the speed with the throttle yet he shook his head in disbelief. I wished he could see it for himself and give me a race yet but I knew that wouldn't happen.

Mr Thomson didn't have a television and I liked to tell him about my favourite programmes which then included Dr Who and Bonanza. Cowboys he understood but time travel was beyond him.

"I remember going to see cowboy movies with Betty, first the silent ones and then the talkies. I loved it when the posses were chasing the baddies across the plains." He started to hum a tune which I didn't recognize but assumed came from a film.

"Why don't you get a TV so you can watch cowboys?" I asked him one day.

"My pension wouldn't stretch to renting one but I have the radio and I like to listen to comedies and the football commentary, especially if the Hibs are playing." He pointed at the brown Bush radio with three white knobs sitting on his sideboard. I liked the radio too but felt sorry he couldn't enjoy the TV.

****

The warning signs were there but I was too young to pick them up. I had just returned from a visit to the fairground in the next town where I had spent all of my pocket money when he called me up from his window. He had been making a big jigsaw of steam locomotive on the dining table in his living room and from time to time I had helped him find where pieces fitted, being a big lover of trains myself. It was an image of a black locomotive emerging from a tunnel belching steam and he had almost finished it when I last visited. When I came into the room this time I saw some pieces of jigsaw strewn on the floor and those on the table messed up. "Did you have an accident?" I asked looking sadly at the virtual train crash.

"Ach, it's a waste of time," he replied in a harsh voice easing himself into his chair. "I've no time for things like that anymore. You'll find the money and the bottle in the kitchen."

His lips tightened as he spoke. I could tell he didn't want to talk about the matter and was worried that he might be angry with me so I set off on my errand.

A few days then passed without him summoning me to his flat. I thought he might have missed me passing so decided to call round unexpectedly. I knocked on the door a few times before he answered. I could hear him loudly muttering as he undid the chain before unlocking the door.

"Oh, it's you. I thought it might have been that nosy nurse again." It was the first time I had seen him without his cap and surprised to see the thick white thatch which it had been hiding.

"Wait there a moment." I could see that he hadn't shaved for a while as he had white stubble on his chin and wondered if he was trying grow a beard like Santa. Returning, he handed me the empty bottle and money without his usual smile. I could smell him from where I was standing; not the usual soap mixed with cologne smell but a sweaty, fetid whiff. When I returned with the fresh bottle he took it from me without comment and closed the door. I felt tears welling in my eyes, feeling that I had lost my friend and ran down the stairs.

I was wandering down our street a few days later, a nutty toasty scent emitting from the nearby brewery, when I saw him leaning out of his window. I skipped up the stairs relieved that he was no longer angry with me but was greeted when the door opened with an upsetting sight.

"Son," he said in a whisper leaning forward, "just take the

bottle to Mr Hunter and he will give you the three pence deposit for it." He was still smelly and his collarless white shirt was stained, and my ten year old self could see that the light had gone out in his eyes.

"Don't you want some more lemonade?" I asked pleadingly.

"No, you treat yourself with the money." He stumbled for a moment before managing to recover himself, and then the door closed.

I felt something was not right and ran home to tell my mum what had happened. At first, she was dismissive.

"He is just being grumpy again. Ignore him."

However, I continued to nag, telling her she needed to do something. Eventually, she relented and took off her apron and went across the road to investigate, with me in tow. She knocked several times on the door and started banging hard when there was no response. Then she began to worry and went downstairs to the neighbour below called Jimmy who had a telephone. I stood nervously outside the door as she rang the local police station. We then waited with the Jimmy in the hallway.

A few minutes later the car arrived and two officers got out and rushed upstairs. They were both big and strong and we watched as they shoulder charged the door and broke in. Returning to the landing, one of the officers told my mum that he was calling an ambulance as they had found Mr Thomson lying with his head in the gas oven but still alive. At first, I was puzzled why Mr Thomson would do something like that but then remembered from a history lesson at school that gas had killed men in the first world war. I started to cry but my mum hugged me and told me that I had saved his life by pestering her to go to his flat.

Mum took me home and from our window we watched the ambulance arrive, blue lights flashing and some time later the ambulance men emerging carrying a stretcher with a prone figure lying on it. This was not the ambulance outing which Mr Thomson had hoped for, I thought.

I kept that lemonade bottle in my bedroom for a long time, hoping that he would come back one day. But I never saw him again. Looking back more than fifty years later, I still feel angry that Mr Thomson was imprisoned above ground having lost his mobility in a war which was not of his asking. I learned years later that he recovered in hospital after the suicide attempt and ended up in a nursing home for war veterans. I like to think of him seeing out his final days in the company of old comrades and with a garden where he could enjoy the sun when it came out. And maybe one day he saw Scalextric cars racing around the track in an advert on TV.

Rob was a civil servant for many years and wrote many policy documents. He took up short story writing to see whether his ability to put things down on paper could be adapted to telling tales. He thinks he's making some progress but has a lot more to learn.

DEAD DREAMS

By Sandeep Kumar Mishra

In his dreams, Rajan searches for the ghosts. He hunts for them, tracing their footsteps in the dirt. He is back in his hometown— he knows these roads. The moonlight shivers on his skin. The crooked streets rattle around him. His heart burns in his chest. Baba, mama. Where are you?

He runs, following the path laid out for him. The streets smell like smoke. Everything is hazy and deserted, shuttered up and locked away. He knows his neighbors behind each door, but no one steps out to help him. They're too scared. Rajan is terrified, too, but he keeps running.

Please, if I could just see you one more time. Baba, Mama.

When he looks up, the ghosts are further away than before. They blur in the distance, like poorly developed photos, but he can still sense the sadness etched upon their faces. Their feet twist backward from their bodies. Bhuta. Spirits. He should have known better— he's been following their trail the wrong way the entire time. He won't ever catch up now.

Grief sweeps over Rajan like a monsoon. He drops to his knees. The ground begins to crumble. A dark pit opens underneath him— a grave, cloying and sticky with the scent of death. The spirits watch from a distance, cold in the low moonlight. Rajan falls.

He wakes up with a jolt. It's still dark outside. Warm air filters in from the cracked window by his cot. The only sound in his cell is his own unsteady breath and what sounds like the rustle of paper. He looks at his journals, but they lie still across the room, untouched.

He looks out the window. Two beady black eyes stare back at him, then rise in the dark, unfurling into an undulating brown body. The snake's tail lashes out and strikes the window. Rajan jumps back, his heart hammering in his chest. The snake hisses, but it sounds more like a shriek of mocking laughter.

He doesn't sleep for the rest of the night.

****

Dawe spills like pale pink soup over the horizon, bringing with it a searing heat that refuses to break. The prisoners queue up to receive sloppy rations of oatmeal ladled into their bowls. The cafeteria smells like vinegar and bleach.

Rajan sits down at a table and pulls out one of his journals. He's made it a point to write every day he's been imprisoned— it's the only thing keeping him sane. A flip of the journal's pages shows his journey: raw confusion at first,legal jargon to lookup later, and then feverish thoughts of revenge as he realizes what has happened. After, his writing shows a dull acceptance of his fate, then a sudden jolt back to confusion as the pandemic hit and the world spun upside down.

He still feels all those things like an ache in the pit of his chest, a heartburn he can't get rid of. Rajan used to take pride in his sensitive emotions. It made him a better poet, after all, and his poetry landed him a teaching position at a prestigious university. Now, though, he wishes he could turn off his mind. There's too much to feel. It's overwhelming.

"Hey." One of the other prisoners, a skull-inked man aptly nicknamed Bones, nudges Rajan's side. "Stop writing, professor. What's the point? None of us are ever getting out of here."

Rajan does not spare him a glance and continues writing. "The words are the point." If he doesn't write, then the words haunt him in the dark, and he doesn't sleep.

Bones grunts. "That's deep, man. I bet if I was that deep, my wife wouldn't have left me."

This is a ritual the prisoners go through daily, sitting around the table and wishing things had gone differently— a storytelling of sorts.

Rajan has heard it all by now. If I hadn't met her… if he hadn't pissed me off so much… if the cops hadn't been nearby that day… Rajan has never played their game. There's no point in wondering about the past. He isn't even sure about enough details about his case to wish differently.

All Rajan knows is this: One minute, he was an esteemed professor travelling internationally to attend a literary seminar. The next, airport security found a bag of white powder in his carry-on, and there was a global pandemic. The world was having a collective panic attack, and his pleas of innocence were lost in the cries of a million others.

Rajan's mouth goes dry just thinking about the horrors of that day. He takes a sip of milk, but it's curdled and stings going down his throat. He hacks up a cough.

Bones leans back. "Hey, get away from me, man. Is that contagious?"

"The sour milk? I hope not." Rajan understands Bones' anxiety. The fear of the plague is almost a second pandemic in and of itself. He sets the cup on the corner of his tray, as if it must be quarantined from the rest.

"Ugh." Bones makes a face. "Why is everything here so rotten?"

"It's a metaphor," Rajan tells him dryly, and they both laugh.

****

Mid-morning, he gets a migraine, which makes him scream and kick his cot in frustration. He's been plagued by headaches his whole life, but they got viciously worse when he came to Australia eight months ago: Something about the climate, he suspects. He's learned that there's nothing to do but wait them out.

Rajan curls up in a corner of the room, his hands wrapped around his knees. White spots dance in his vision. It feels like a hammer is raining blows down on the back of his skull.

When things got this bad, his wife used to soothe him with a cool compress, but now she's a continent away. He passes out with her name on his tongue.

In his hazy, pain-filled sleep, he sees a snake. He can tell by the markings that it's the same one from the previous night. Mottled spots of green blot the snake's body like mold. No, not mold— it reminds Rajan of the diagrams of the COVID-19 virus he and the other prisoners were shown at the beginning of the pandemic.

The snake hisses at him. Rajan is distantly aware that this is a dream, so he does not flinch. The desert blurs around him. The prison is at his back. He's outside. He's free, if he can just get past the snake in his path.

Rajan picks up a stick from the ground, intending to shoo the snake away. Before he can, the snake shrieks and flails, its tail lashing on the ground. Rajan jumps back. The snake hurls itself towards him. He raises the stick and clubs it over the head. Its scales brush his wrist. He feels a pinch of pain. He pulls away and strikes it again. It keens, wild and pained. Adrenaline floods Rajan's veins. He strikes the snake for a third time. It lies still.

Breathing hard, Rajan looks down at his wrist. Two pin-point pricks of fang-bite are embedded in his skin. Poison seeps slowly through his veins. Dizziness overwhelms him, and he collapses.

He wakes up smothered in sheets from head to toe, like a funeral shroud.

****

The rest of the week flits by like a ghost in the mist. Time blurs, and Rajan struggles to find things to record in his journal. It's just another day after day after day. What is there to write about when everyone is trapped, when nothing changes? He knows vaguely that this is momentous, that the world has never seen a pandemic of this magnitude, but he's so isolated in the prison that he can't even conceptualize how the outside world is changed.

He is starting to forget the details of his family's faces. He draws awkward, crooked pictures of them in his journal. Does his father wear two rings or one? Does his mother have a mole under her right eye or left? It strikes Rajan with a deep, tolling sadness that he will never again be able to look at them and remember.

With nothing else to do, Rajan starts recording his dreams. The doctor prescribed him sleeping pills to help with the migraines and insomnia and they do help, but they make him dizzy, thick-limbed and unable to differentiate wake and sleep. In this half-twilight, he writes:

October 18, 2020. The ghosts came to visit me again. This time, it was my children. They danced around me in a circle, chanting, "Baba's dead! Baba's dead!"

I tried to tell them that I wasn't dead, that I was just away temporarily, but they couldn't hear or see me. I tried to embrace them, ruffle their hair, but I couldn't touch them. It was as if I was invisible or a ghost. Am I becoming a ghost?

My feet are straight, and bhuta are restless, transient things. I never move. I am stuck. I hate being so stuck.

October 19, 2020. Last night, I saw the snake. The same snake I always do. I killed the snake. But the snake returns. It bites itself— a perfect, pure, ouroboros. It behaves like it also wants to die. I don't know how to feel about this. The snake returns. The snake returns.

The rest of the entry trails off into unintelligibility, marked by a spot of sleepy drool at the edge of the page.

****

"What's up, dude?" Bones prods Rajan's shoulder. They're in the exercise yard, Rajan crouching to pick up a dumbbell bar, Bones watching to make sure he doesn't injure himself. "You look even more depressed than usual, which is saying something."

Rajan focuses his efforts on squatting, then lifting the bar over his head. His muscles burn, but it feels good to sweat. "Nothing. I'm fine."

"Really?" Bones arches an eyebrow. "You look like you're about to pass out."

"I am not—" A burst of light-headedness flows through Rajan. He sways unsteadily on his feet and sets the dumbbell down with a thunk. "I am not going to pass out," he says, panting.

"Seriously, professor, you're worrying me." Bones offers him a water bottle, which Rajan gratefully accepts. "Is it the nightmares? Are they getting worse?"

Rajan blinks. Water drips down his chin. "How did you know?"

"You cry in your sleep." At Rajan's expression, Bones rushes to reassure him. "We all get the bad dreams, dude. We've all been through something heavy. If anyone judges you for it, I'll beat them up."

"Thanks," Rajan says, flattered by the offer. He wipes sweat off his forehead. "I think… I might be cursed. I don't know." He gestures to his chest. "All my emotions are like water, filling me up, drowning me. There's only so much grief a person can take."

Bones sits next to him. "What do you see in the dreams? You don't have to tell me if you don't want to."

"A snake," Rajan says, holding up his hands. "About this big. We fight. I kill it. The snake returns."

Bones scratches his head. "The same dream? Every night?"

Rajan shrugs. "Pretty much."

"Cool," says Bones. "In my dreams, my wife always yells at me all the time." Rajan laughs humourlessly. "If you had the same dream every night, a spirit was haunting you. You needed to do something to appease it."

"Like what?"

"Well, leave bowls of honey and milk outside for the fairies to eat, but you can't do that here.

Maybe just do something different to help it out?

Hmm.

"Bones taps his hand against the barbell. "Saying that aloud, it all sounds pretty nutty."

Rajan gestures to the prison yard, to the barb-wire walls and the world at large, where panic and a pandemic consume them all.

"If you ask me, anything's worth a try."

"Or ask your doctor to double your prescription."

"No, thanks. If I take any more sleeping pills, I might never wake up again." The thought had been appealing, at times, but Rajan can't go through with that. He has to find his way back to India, to his wife and to his children, to his parent's ghosts and graves. He has to believe that someday, this will end. Giving up means he will end.

****

Rajan takes no sleeping pills that night. He lies on his cot, his arms folded over his chest, and watches the moonlight seep like spoiled milk through the window. Some part of him thinks the snake might come to find him while he is awake, but the desert outside his window remains bleak and empty. In the end, he has to go to it, instead.

He closes his eyes. His breathing is soft and steady. He slips into sleep and dreams.

Here he is again. The jail behind him, the snake in front of him. Imprisonment or death. Are those his only options? Is he supposed to give up and let the snake poison him? Rajan refuses to believe it is so.

The snake bares its fangs, which curve like crescent moons in the light. Rajan picks up the stick. The wood is familiar in his hands, grooved from his grip.

"Back off," he tells the snake. It hisses at him. "I mean it."

The snake lunges for him. Rajan dodges away, swiping the stick out to protect his bare feet.

"What do you want from me? Just leave me alone!"

The snake writhes and coils. Its tail thumps in the dirt again. Rajan hits it with the stick. It howls.

This is his dilemma, the problem he's figured out over many nights of mystic battle: He can wound the snake, but whenever he closes in for the killing blow, it finds a way to bite him. Slaughtering it only results in both of them dying.

Do something different. Break the cycle. Bones' voice whispers in the back of Rajan's head. Rajan backs away. The snake follows. Blood drips from its abdomen.

"Stop," Rajan says. "I don't want to hurt you." The snake ignores him. It seems compelled to attack. Its black eyes fix on the weapon in his hand.

So Rajan sets the stick down.

His heart is pounding in his chest. He raises his hands above his head. "See?" he says, mouth dry. "I mean it."

The snake rises up, twists its head to consider him. Its eyes reflect the white-chip light of the stars above.

"Go," Rajan says. "You're released. You don't have to die to be free."

The snake places its body back on the flat ground, as if it is bowing to him. Then it slithers off into the desert, leaving soft plumes of dust in its wake. Rajan drops his hands, breathing heavily. He takes a step forward into the night. Nothing stops him. For once, there are no ghosts, no migraines, no spirit-snakes waiting to strike. He is free.

****

The next morning, a guard comes to visit his cell, rapping loudly on the bars.

"Hey. Wake up."

Rajan hasn't slept. This time, it wasn't insomnia, but indecision: He is burdened by his choice to let the snake go free. What has he set loose? The nightmare has so warped his life that he can't help but imagine it will impact the waking world, too. For all his metaphors, for all his knowledge of spirits and curses and dreamscapes, he doesn't know what he's done.

"Get going," the guard snaps. "You're leaving."

Rajan blinks, sits up. "Leaving?"

"In three hours."

He almost doesn't want to ask. It's too much to hope for. "Where— where am I going?"

"I dunno. Back to wherever you came from, I guess," the guard sneers, but Rajan barely registers the jab. He's going to get out.

He glances down at the page in his journal, where he has written the first scrawling lines of a poem: today I did not kill the snake / I set it free / it will return to the wild / I will wait for its mercy / and it will return to me.

He asks, though he already suspects the answer, "Why?"

"Prison's full— we need more space than usual because of the pandemic. You're a minor offender. Your sentence was shortened. Congratulations." The guard tosses a piece of paper at him, presumably some sort of official court document.

"Pack your stuff."

Three hours later, he's out the door.

Two guards accompany him on either side, their nightsticks swinging. A car idles a few yards away. Rajan breathes in the sweet desert air. The heat doesn't bother him, and his migraine has faded. Clouds of dust bloom like flowers. The world is still. Even the tumbleweed has stopped its travels to watch him. It would make a good setting for a poem, Rajan thinks.

As he takes his first steps as a free man, a snakeskin snaps beneath his shoe.

Sandeep Kumar Mishra is a bestseller author, an outsider artist, a poet, a teacher and the poetry editor at Indian Poetry Review. He has received a number of awards for his writing.

FOREVER I DROWN

by Kieran Rollin

I wake up, if this is even awake, to colicky crying from the cot. Down the hall, through the wall, alive and incessant need. Kate kicks me under the covers and I squash the tip of my tongue between my teeth to feel something. Pain, wet hot, blood. I am still human.

Barely, but still here.

I tilt the bottle and brush the rubber nipple against his lips, but he cries harder. Am I holding him right? I walk through the night of the living room with the bundle of him curled in my arms, shuddering between crying fits. I sleep on the chair; he sleeps on my chest. When Kate wakes up before the sun she looks inscrutably at the fresh carpet of snow outside, blueglow in the pre-dawn. I tell her I am too tired but she urges me with a look, to leave the house, to recover, to rediscover mountain air. The feeling appeals. We are both cabin fevered. Drey arrives in his pick-up and I throw my stuff in the back. We drive up into the canyons leaving Kate and the baby behind.

They are as free and scary as childhood, the canyons that is. We lived in Texas, Kate and I, briefly, for work and I missed the mountains. I missed old friends and familiar roads without pavements and sorry, bare lawns that stretched from the asphalt to the front doors. A landscape without mountains is like a house without a roof. The pick-up grips the snow now, the slope of land expands white forever, and the canyon grows without ever seeming to get closer. Even in the moment, I am nostalgic for all of it. I watch the land move behind us as Drey talks.

We park and climb the rest on foot.

The snow is deeper here, a fresh layer of powder lifted and tossed in spurts by a listless wind as we trudge onwards to a fool's hunt. The leopard supposed in those mountains, passed down to us by a couple of sophomore kids back when we were in middle school. Told again on porches, in the smoke of summer, in the seated roister of bars, and in the drunken twilight of wedding parties.

We walk forever, from peak to peak across the saddles, keeping the yawn of black rock visible to our right where the river cuts through the gorge, hunting a leopard of myth.

There is a man near-drowned in the river. I drag him out, grasping him tenuously by the arms of his sodden jacket and shiver as the cold cuts its way through me.

I wake up, if this is even awake, to colicky crying from the cot. Need bolts into a room, our room, like a hunted deer. Need, need, need. Kate kicks me and I barely feel it. I squash the tip of my tongue between teeth to feel something. Pain, wet, hot blood. I am still human.

Drey fills the kitchen, high-school lineman turned adult bear.

He stoops instinctively. The sky has fallen, piled white on the land outside and on the windowsill. The kitchen is white tile and white cabinets. The percolator makes white noise. I could fade away.

Kate walks in as the coffee clicks, she must have gotten him back to sleep.

Drey grins at her. "You didn't have to dress up for me, Kate."

She ignores him at first, pours the coffee into one of the prepared cups, tiny hands beneath the folds of her dressing gown, then she raises her glare at him. It drifts past him tepidly. Blotchy chin, wearied eyes, sickly-sheen cheeks. She leaves the other two cups empty and walks into a corner, leaning against the refrigerator with the coffee held against her chest.

"Coffee's done."

It should be a threat, but, in her weariness, it lacks the venom. Drey takes it as a joke.

"No, no, no, not for me." He reaches for the box of Win Mags I've put on the table and pockets them. Drey moves loudly, talks loudly; his insulated jacket announces every gesture and shift with plastic thunder. "We'll just pack your boy up and be out of your hair." He looks at her straggly up-do with the wild flyaways and she arches both eyebrows back at him.

I hunt him out of the kitchen, laces unfastened, carrying my coat, trying to trick myself into excitement, trying to give Kate clear reprieve, silence, emptiness, baby on standby. Hurried and on instinct I kiss her goodbye. It catches us both by surprise. She is gummy with sleep-mouth and unbrushed teeth, tasting of coffee, but the old life stirs in her widened eyes and I can feel it too. It is a rescue of sorts; I can't tell who is saving who.

I pull the man out of the water, Drey grabbing me by the belt and pulling me back so that my trousers slip down and I tumble back onto the icy snow bare-ass. The man lands on my chest, purple lipped. He could be sleeping, I roll him onto his back. He was only under the water briefly but memories of learning CPR in high school flit through my head. Tilt the head back, open the mouth, I think Drey was in the same class, check that the tongue hasn't rolled back, the doll had a plastic sheen, seal the mouth with your own, and a ridiculous red erotic hole of a mouth, and blow two full breaths. I move towards the man and think strangely of the globby kiss with Kate that morning.

I wake up, if this is even awake, to colicky crying from the cot. Through the hall, down the walls, need, need, need. Kate kicks me and I barely feel it. I barely bite my tongue, blood barely wells around my teeth, I am barely human.

We've been climbing upwards in a quiet, slow slalom through the trees. I've known him since middle school, quiet with Drey's as good as quiet with myself. He leads and I trail in his giant footholes. Just the cool crepitation of footsteps on snow talking for us and the whispery freshness in the air. My breath mists and wets my nose whenever a stray wind blows back at me.

But the cold only serves to numb the numbness. I am feverish without fever. Sunk beneath my own skin, other bodied, other minded, I am

Tired.

All I want

Is sleep.

We have wound our way to the edge of the canyon. The glaucoma sky touches heaven to earth and the lands falls away into a black scar, scabrous shelves of rock stepping down towards the river that cuts through everything and eats the snow and ice from its banks.

Drey spots it at the same time as I do, the dark lump in the water and the current frothing around it. It could be a beaver, or a bear cub, or…

After a beat of stiltedness, my stomach lurches and Drey curses. He moves for the path that steers down, I move closer to the edge, gauge the distance. The river is a wire, the trees are mossy clots. I walk out onto nothing and drop down onto a large clear outcrop. My knees take the landing and shout. I sidle to the edge again and find a smaller shelf about twelve feet down. I step out, I drop. I bend my knees, chest pressed against the thickness of my stiff jacket. The rifle, slung around my back, clatters against the stone. The air feels thinner. I do this again and again. I fly. The moments without gravity are new life. Drey shouts above me but I am too alive to care. I slip on one of the edges as I am just about to jump, and my heart seizes with adrenaline. I lean backwards, the stone catches my coat and lifts it upwards scraping my back as I slide down, panicking for purchase. I skid twenty feet or so before I land in a seat of rock. Cross one of my nine off the list. I let myself breathe, laugh without humour, fix my coat and go again.

The ground comes too soon. I don't know if I will ever feel as close to God again.

****

I wake up, if this is even awake, to colicky crying from the cot. Down the hall, through the wall, falling through the bottom of the bed. Kate kicks me and wakes me from a half-dreamed vertigo. I squash the tip of my tongue between teeth for luck.

I plant my feet by the bed before getting up fully, letting realness creep back into me.

Back and forth, I walk between the kitchen and the living room, shrugging him up and down, whispering 'little man' over and over into the top of his head. His cries corkscrew through his tiny body. His round fists clench and bowed legs kick, his face grows red. Hot tears leak from scrunched eyes. I ratchet in the verisimilitude of him, I ache. We watch the sky fall. Whisper white curtains swirling down through the night, frostmoths drifting out of the black and melting on the glass. He is between crying fits, catching his breath. I could bury him in the snow.

****

I wake up, if this is even awake, to colicky crying from the walls. Growing beyond the cot, the house: a tumescent need. Kate kicks me in the teeth to feel something and blood wells, wet and warm. I am still human.

"Hattie's pregnant."

Drey says it without taking his eyes off the road as it takes us into the mountains.

I want to grab the wheel and run us into the drifts, save us both.

****

I wake up, if this is even awake, to colicky crying from the cot. Down the mountains, through the earth, cries tremble. A present cry, an ancient cry, primeval need. Kate kicks me through time. I squash the tip of my tongue between teeth. I am cold.

I lie down, flatten my body across the ice flow with toes dug into the frozen riverbank for purchase. The movement scoops snow into my collar and shrugs it down against my chest. There is a sound of cracking, swallowed by the rush of water,

I can't tell if I imagined it, or if it was a rustle of coat, or the snow inside it. Or the ice underneath me.

The man is a head of wet black curls, urgent eyes, purple shaking lips, a shoulder out of the water, one arm somehow gripping the slippery ice and stopping the river from carrying him away to bounce him through the rocks. As I stretch out for him, he lunges at me, the hand that had been underwater is a baby's fist crippled pink with cold. He lifts up and then falls backward. I grab his arms - forearms, wrists, hands - and we both slip. The ice cracks under my chest, dissolves, sinks into the water. My toes tense, my legs tense and they root me to the banks whilst the rest of me slips into the river.

The cold, the shock of it. Air leaks from me in little bubbles, tickling my cheeks, moving past me to the surface. I hold onto the man, by the fingertips, everything stretched. The gravity of him pulls me deeper, threatening to untether me and carry me into the sway.

The river, surging on the surface, seems peaceful from below. It is my ceiling, now. The sky is my floor, vaulted cathedral walls of the canyon stretching between, like an inverted Sistine Chapel. There are stones at the bottom of the riverbed, and a half-buried Miller can. I am losing air, still. Water seduces, pressing against my mouth, persistent and patient. If the universe blinked then, I would be preserved in that moment, on the inside of its eyelid, underwater, airless, ageless, staring at stones and silt and rubbish. God and Adam, frozen in paint, forever losing their grasp on one another.

A hand clasps around the back of my belt and I am pulled back ferociously. I surface in a tumult of breath and wet chill and Drey speaking guttural through gritted teeth, "I got you. I got you. Come on. Not today man. I got you."

I cannot feel my fingers, but somehow the man and I still have a hold.

****

I wake up, if this is even awake, to colicky crying from the cot. Down the hall, through the wall, alive and incessant need. Kate licks her paws on the pillow, her leopard eyes grey in the dark. I yell for help and the river floods my mouth. Warm, it tastes like blood.

We had always wanted kids.

I am in the living room. I am stood here and I am not. Tired does that. Splinters me into fragments floating just beneath the surface; they drift like collagen flecks across the eyes. Boiled tasteless eyes.

Here – following the stretch of the black canyon, along its snowy top, between naked aspens and cottonwoods feathered by rime ice. Stood still sky, stood still me.

Here - in a warm bed with a stone wife, chasing sleep.

Here – in the kitchen feeling hollowed, rubbing the back of a life that is half mine yet slowly eating the whole of me, watching the snow. Looking over the pristine blankness on luminescent back yards: the frozen corpses of forgotten basketballs, barbeques, plant pots, a swingset and trampoline.

Here – in a pick-up, the heater gushing stuffy air around the cab, driving up into that great white sea.

Everything white. Trees. Ground. Sky. Winter in Colorado is one of those existential moments in an old cartoon, where the colour leaks and the scenery disappears and the mouse is just running through white. Dodging the eraser on the end of a drawn pencil that's trying to scratch out its little cartoon mouse outlines. Trying to keep the last of its colour.

"Hattie's pregnant."

Drey says it without taking his eyes off the road. We're climbing the trail now, through uneven mud and frozen banks of snow; the pick-up rocks and roils, jumping us in our seats.

"No shit." I realise the dryness of my tone and correct it. "Big Daddy Drey."

He grins, glances at me, his voice is wistful, "Big Daddy Drey." The grin slants a little and he taps the steering wheel. He chews a thought, I know his moods as he knows my own. I ignore him and let him work through it. He relaxes and the silence eases back into the cab.

"Think today's gonna be our day?"

He smiles wide. "Hey, anything's possible, right?"

"Kellem swears he saw it."

Drey scoffs, then laughs. "Kellem's full of it. Remember when he swore he made it with that girl two grades up? And she found out?"

I shake my head, smiling. I'd forgotten that. The tiny city boy with the big mouth and slick haircut hustled by a group of girls. "She really ripped into him."

Drey laughs again. "He didn't know which way to sit for a month. Still doesn't."

Poor Kellem. He'd moved to Grand Junction as a kid but he was still a transplant, still talked funny. He didn't understand the leopard, not properly.

It was an in-joke for us natives, a rite of passage, a dream, a captive childhood. Our Peter Pan. Those snow leopards released by a drunk from Denver Zoo back in the fifties vivified through whispers and rumour and myth. They crossed the Rockies, they lived in the sewers, they were spotted in playing fields and in backyards, they stole pets from their kennels and hutches. We wished them into the Black Canyon. A blend of adolescent camping trips and hunts: bourbon, gun oil and smoky rabbit meat cooked in hot black skillets. The snow leopard loomed through dreams, moved through waters, timeless.

"You'll make a great dad."

"Yeah?" He shifts in his seat and rolls his hands on the wheel, thumbs hooked underneath. "It's just-" he shrugs, "you know?"

I nod my head, but it is lost in the shaking of the cab.

The drowned man coughs water. His eyes bulge open and hands claw at his throat, we have brought him back to life to suffocate. Drey lifts him by the shoulder and we push him onto his side away from us. The black curls on the back of his head shiver. He heaves in a breath. Once, twice.

Silence.

Kieran Rollin writes short stories with a focus on dark themes and the inner psyche, weaving in elements of surrealism and horror. He is a proud Barnsley lad, born-and-bred, and is inspired to give the page over to working-class people and places.

FLASH FICTION

THE PROPOSAL

By Anna Ross

When I stepped outside on Wednesday morning, feeling the weight of the ongoing week on my shoulders, the last thing I expected was a proposal of marriage. I got one though.

Albert had come and stepped right in front of me effectively blocking the path and demanding my full attention. There was clear hope in those eyes and it didn't seem like he was joking. "So…will you?"

I just stared. "I…what?"

He cleared his throat trying to look more proper, which was difficult, considering his out-of-place uniform.

"Will you be my wife?" He awkwardly went down on one knee almost falling over. I bit my lip.

"I'm afraid I can't."

He blinked, looking genuinely taken aback. "But…why?" He scrambled to his feet. "We love each other."

I gave him a supportive smile resting a hand on his shoulder. "I know but I'm already married." I held up my ring and wiggled my fingers.

"I can get you a ring. A better ring."

"I don't even think I could take this one off," I said a little wistfully. I had gained significant weight in the years since my marriage and never been able to fully bounce back no matter how many magazine diets I followed. "But that's not really the problem. The problem is I have a husband."

"But he's not here."

Now that was true. He was off doing 'important' work in Japan. There is no winning when your husband is high up in the charity sector. If you argue against anything you come out looking like the bad guy.

"You can be married to two people."

I laughed. He wasn't technically wrong, there were places you could go to marry multiple people but none of them were within driving distance of Devon.

"I can handle one husband but not two. I'm sorry," I said in a gentle yet firm tone. "But I cannot marry you."

Seeing that this was indeed my final answer his face crumpled and tears filled those big blue eyes. He looked for all the world like he was going to start crying in the middle of the driveway.

My heart ached and I made a snap decision. "Alright, alright, I'll marry you."

"You will?"

I pulled him into my arms smacking a kiss against his rosy

cheeks and wiping away his tears. "Yes, of course."

He gave a smile that made me feel as if the sun had just come out. "Thank you, mummy."

Anna Ross lives in North Yorkshire in the UK and works as a university administrator. Her short stories have been published across a range of anthologies. She enjoys reading and writing poems and stories of all shapes and sizes as well as going on adventures with her D&D group.

THE RELEASING

By Fiona Ritchie Walker

In my hands, a thousand miles of air. Hard to imagine this scrap of beak and feathers shuns dry land, skims the tips of ocean waves. I hold the tiny storm petrel close to my face, breathe in musk.

Sweet like your perfume.

In the air, the recorded call is drawing the birds to land. It happens every year, after the summer solstice. Close to midnight when there's enough dark smudging the sky. The wardens say it doesn't hurt the birds, caught in the soft net, then quickly placed in cotton bags and taken to the hut for ringing.

You saw this island on the map. It was your dream to come here.

Today I saw a yacht skim out from the harbour towards the horizon, felt the current swirl around my bare feet, unsteadying me with its invisible pull.

I didn't refund your ferry ticket. I know you'd laugh, say, it's only paper, but I have it here, in the breast pocket of my jacket.

I was heading for the room you booked, with the window full of sky, when the warden invited me to help. I carried the bird so carefully.

I would love you to feel this heartbeat.

As soon as I saw it, I felt love again. Just a tiny stirring, like wings. I watched skilled fingers secure the ring round the storm petrel's leg.

Like the silver circle I placed on your finger.

The warden leads me towards the shore. I carry the bird in soft hands.

The tiny body is warm, as you were, when I sat by your bed that last time.

I breathe in musk, let my fingers open. Feel the flutter of a life, leaving. Your voice in my head.

It's time for the releasing.

A tiny silhouette shows dark as it flies across the moon.

Fiona Ritchie Walker is a Scottish poet, now based in England, who began writing flash fiction during lockdown. Volunteering at the bird observatory on Fair Isle – the UK's more remote inhabited island – inspired her story. Find her on Twitter @guttedherring

SECOND-BEST HUSBAND

By Chris Cottom

Agnes has remained barren these eight years. I tell myself we are sufficient for one another, that not all wives are called to motherhood, yet sorrow settles over our union like a shroud. She continues to give herself to me as often as my loins require, but more, I fear, from obedience than desire.

We pass our days in the fine sash-windowed house she'd shared with her first husband, one in a row of such residences bestowed on the nation's sea captains by His Gracious Majesty, King Charles. Naturally I, a mere Admiralty lawyer, am pleased to dwell in this splendour beside the great waterway on which our city's proud history is founded. Yet I would exchange it for the lowliest hovel, were it with my beloved.

Agnes takes to picking at her food and often frets at our fireside while winter howls its storms through which greater men than I battle their creaking vessels. At such times she'll ask me to carry her rosewood writing box to her parlour. There she will remove its key from the locket around her neck, bid me to leave her, and pass an hour or more in doleful remembrance.

She falls silent when I ask, so I can only surmise the box's contents: her garter from her first wedding perhaps, pressed flowers from her bouquet, a bundle of Captain Robert's letters from across the globe, pieces of his linen, aged and yellowed but unwashed since last he'd worn them before being laid to rest in the Sargasso Sea. Would that she might accord her present husband the esteem with which she cherishes such keepsakes of her first!

On Lammas Day, Agnes takes sick and remains in her chamber, falling within a fortnight into a fevered slumber, her face grey and her brow damp with the glint of ague. The surgeon calls but counsels only that we must wait. I spend the hours praying that my dear wife's soul will pass smoothly into the eternal care of Our Lord. I try not to picture her resting again in the arms of Captain Robert.

As morning gilds the skies, I awake in my chair to find her finally at peace. After her maids have washed her, I bend to kiss her cold lips. I open my pocket knife, clasp her locket, snip its black silk ribbon and draw it gently through the fair tresses spread across the bolster.

I take Agnes's rosewood box and carry it under my arm along the Embankment. At Westminster Bridge I cross to the middle, rest the box before me on the parapet, take its key from my waistcoat pocket and unlock it. My fingers tremble as I raise the lid, ready to cast Agnes's few sad mementos of Captain Robert into the river.

Yet the sole items inside are a white christening robe, a bone-handled silver rattle and, tied with faded pink thread, a tiny lock of thistle-soft golden hair.

Chris lives near Macclesfield and is a retired insurance copywriter. He won the 2021 Retreat West Flash Fiction Prize and in the early 1970s lived next door to JRR Tolkien.

VOICES

By R.F.Marazas

She called me one morning and said, "Don't call me. Don't ever call me again."

So I didn't, even though I liked her voice. She had started out pretending to be angry (I noticed that right away) but wound down to a soft honeyed murmur after the first three words, and then she paused after the last five, breathed a sigh, and hung up, gently.

After a week passed she called, pretend angry again, but I detected honest puzzlement in her lovely voice, and she asked why I hadn't called her. I pointed out in my silky morning baritone that she warned me not to call her, not ever again.

She denied this, but not very convincingly, so I insisted. We sparred a while yet both kept our voices reasonable and calm. No hint of shrillness. Stalemated when I refused to agree with her version, she hung up again, no less gently.

She called a month later and cried, although that did nothing to detract from the thrilling sound of her voice. Was I punishing her? I was not, I protested. Then why wouldn't I call her? Tell the truth, none of this you-told-me-not-to. I gave three excellent, logical reasons, enunciating each word clearly. She had originally dialed the wrong number. Therefore I didn't know who she was. Lastly, I had no idea what her phone number was.

She stopped crying. "Oh," she said. After a long pause, during which I enjoyed listening to her breathing as much as her voice, she said, "I like your voice."

"I love your voice," I said.

We're both buying cell phones so we can continue to listen to each other every day until we meet and marry next spring.

R.F. Marazas is the author of several published stories including The Toast Family's Magic Radio, Pelham's Saturday Morning Frolics, The Duck, and Beyond My Window. He has been writing creative fiction for 60 years and lives in Belvidere in the USA. He loves to write about slightly odd situations.

TILL DEATH DO US PART

By Holly Hamp

I have been a secret to the world for a very long time, but now I am yours, and only yours at last. Sometimes my mind is curious to understand why we couldn't be to the known to public. After all, my devotion to you has been nothing short of biblical. I am sure there will be those who think me naïve in my actions, to be so intoxicated by you. By what? A man of such power, who transfixed those around him with his passionate words, how could I not fall captive also. When we first met, I was merely past my age of sweet adolescence, and I knew then that I would forever be by your side. I have heard the comments that they make of me, 'inconsequential and feather-brained' that pompous photographer of yours remarked. You told me once exactly what I wanted to hear, that I caught you candidly far better than Hoffman ever could. I didn't know if you were telling the truth or not, but I have never forgotten it. Undoubtedly, you have been cruel and bitter with me at times. It has caused me to suffer greatly, but still, I come flocking back to you like an overly attached youngling, unwilling to fledge its nest. Making ours a story of dedication, resilience, and vigour these past sixteen years.

Behind all the shadows of my own self-doubt there were exceptions to my distaste for being hidden and isolated all these years. There were times I didn't care at all, I was glad to know I would be kept as your secret, that I was helping to aid your cause further, people would see you as the pure visionary that you are. A chaste man with one focus. One goal. I am proud to have been an instrument of your orchestration in any way possible. I played my part well.

These last few hours have been all I ever desired, and I am so grateful that I could be with you to share this moment together.

As we are sequestered here, the invasion is drawing in ever closer and the heavy artillery above is weighing us down with its dull but alarming thuds. It is getting louder with each passing day, so we have very little choice left.

I must heartlessly admit that seeing your beloved dog leave us gave me a great sense of pleasure, though I was not pleased to see her suffer as she did. The pills caused a great deal of convulsion along with a struggle to catch her last escaping breath. You say however that the opioids will help, and we will feel no pain like she did.

I'm not afraid at all of what comes after because I have been here before, so no, I am not afraid. I only ask that the Lord be merciful and that both our souls be saved. Swallow quick and let it consume us, as you have me.

'Bereit?' Ready?

'Bereit, Mein Führer.'

Holly Hamp is a short story and flash fiction writer who lives in Harrogate, Yorkshire, UK with her partner Adam and their Alaskan Malamute called Enzo.

A PATIENT LISTENER

By June Barnes-Rowley

She details each and every event in her day. Only his eyes respond.

Once robust with a domineering personality, he lies locked in a paralysed body, robbed of speech.

His wife of thirty-five years visits daily. "Remember when we'd sit on the terrace and I'd tell you about my day, dear?"

Nurses in the corridor cannot hear her softly spoken words. Only he can hear.

"Shut up! Stop prattling on about nothing. That's what you used to yell at me." A sweet smile. "Now look at you; hanging on my every word."

Behind the smile, her eyes reveal her triumph.

June Barnes-Rowley (JB) grew up in a small Australian town and now lives in Melbourne. As a child, she spent many hours in the hayshed reading books by authors such as Enid Blyton and Charles Dickens. JB writes the Dusty Kent Murder Mystery series under the penname Brigid George.

READING IN WINTER

By David Davies

He stopped brushing his teeth to look out of the bathroom window. Snow had fallen overnight and settled on the Chinese Windmill Palm. Thirty years before when it was planted, there was a fashion for the exotic, but now he wondered if it looked a bit incongruous.

He realised the grey skies over the allotments were encouraging negative thoughts, conspiring to stifle his imagination. He reminded himself that in the summer, the tree with a backdrop of blue sky created a different mood.

On those days, a novel by Paul Bowles could transport him to a hotel just off the souk in Tangiers, or V.S. Naipaul to Trinidad. Hemingway...that could be Havana, Spain, Africa, anywhere. The tree stimulated his imagination. In winter, it reminded him that there were more exotic and exciting places in the world, though he may never see them. That thought stopped him in his tracks.

The tree had caused arguments with his wife. As it grew bigger, she complained that it blocked out the light in the conservatory. 'What's the point of a conservatory without light?' She hated the tree and would have preferred something smaller, something scented. Neither did she like his choice of colonial style wicker chairs. His Somerset Maughams, as he liked to call them.

He was staring into the garden, completely lost in thought. It was the sudden realisation that he was seventy three years old, and most definitely in the last quarter of his life.

Retired now, but he had worked all his life in the warehouse of a book distribution firm in the city. He was never an ambitious man, but always a reader, and there were perks with the job. Staff got first dibs on 'damaged' and 'seconds', so he never considered leaving. Why would he?

Since retirement, he had slipped into the habit of reading in bed, getting up a bit later and eating breakfast alone. His wife was younger and still working. She always left early.

He was feeling uneasy. He had started to see the tree as some kind of replacement for reality. He had been dreaming life away beneath the palm's shade.

When his wife got home, there was no sign of him. On the table, propped against the still warm tea pot was a slim paperback book. As I Walked Out One Midsummer

Morning by Laurie Lee. Stuck to the bottom of the book was a yellow Post It note with words clearly designed to irk.

At last you are free, to cut down my tree.

She read the note with a weary dismissal. 'Not again…God he loves a drama'. She carried the book to the drawer where she kept all the others. On top of the pile was last winter's farewell. Primo Levi's If Not Now, When? A couple more years and the drawer wouldn't close. She wouldn't ring the tree surgeon just yet. She would give it a couple of hours. That was usually enough.

David has had several pieces published in anthologies in Britain, the US, Australia, and Japan. He prefers short fiction and poetry and reached the last four in an international flash competition run by STAUNCH in 2020.

Poetry

FULL MOON

By Junia Dia

All eyes turn to the full moon

and I think of the months

I would live without you.

At first, counting, one, two,

the belly of the autumn leaf

facing the sky, before it touches

the cold ground.

The shedding of the seasons

as close to me as the dry skin

on my thumb, hardening

before it leaves.

Until slowly —

like sunflowers craning east,

I would remember you.

Each memory sown wilfully

into the verdant expanse

that sees the sun rise daily

on the field.

Junia Dia is a poet based in London. Her inspirations include the works of E. Bishop and A. Carson. Her triumph in The Anansi Archive poetry competition has inspired her to keep writing and challenge herself.

COUNTERPOINT

By B.C. Burnett

(Both parts to be read simultaneously)

Voice 1 (The Classical)	Voice 2 (The Romantic)
As the crystal orbs turn	Out of mist, the storm churns:
emergent harmonies arise,	a turbid elemental appetite,
giving rhythm to creation:	giving motion fire and mixing
a rule to measure man and cage	purified passion, disordered flame –
an order, mathematical –	emotions tangled, tangible –
the purest structure is devised –	the truest picture of man's plight
bright limpidity as tightest sound,	lies in pity of the animal ground:
celestial balance, eternal conjunction,	flesh and fur in essential union,
white and gold of Ionian mode;	red and black Stendhalian code;
heaven's law calls and	chaos bore all and
awaits our refrain.	takes us back again.

B.C. Burnett lives between London and Copenhagen. He recently completed a PhD on the philosophy of memory, and is interested in the development of systems of ideas and in the problems of memory.

UNDERESTIMATED KNIFE

By Lydia Durrant

Quiet and unassuming

Mistaken for kind

The blanks are filled

No blood is spilled

Except for in my mind

In my mind I cut you down

My words leave you gasping

But all you see is a girl

Quiet and unassuming

Originally from the North East of England, Lydia has been writing on and off for years but only recently begun to submit her work. This is her first published poem.

THE PHONE CALLS

By April Miller

The phone calls,

My world sent spinning,

Tears falling.

My breath labouring.

Heart breaking

Pain in simply living.

Dad departing.

The phone calls,

Smiles all around.

New heart beating.

New life breathing.

A nephew to delight in.

The phone calls,

Happiness spreading

Wedding bells ringing

Hearts leaping

For a brother marrying

The phone calls

Sharp blades shredding

Soul screaming

Metal twisting

My baby bleeding

The phone calls

Emergency lights flashing

Machines beeping

Deep deep weeping

My princess almost permanently sleeping.

The phone calls....

April is originally from Yorkshire and is inspired by inspiration family and the events we all enjoy or endure in an average lifetime. She likes to write about the familiar.

LETTER

By Max Williams

Inside a corner of my head,

I found a letter yet unread.

The cursive writing seemed to say

That I should throw myself away.

I burned that letter charcoal black,

But still the thought kept coming back.

The paper gone, there still survived

The strange solution it prescribed

In haunting echoes deep inside;

A virus gnawing at my pride.

It's weakened me a bit each day

And makes me feel I cannot stay.

I scream, I cry, I plead, I shout

But still can't block the damn words out.

Max is a writer of both words and music from Devon, UK, with an inclination to the old-fashioned. His first poetry book Love Is Not Always Kind And Sweet is available now.

THE GARDEN

By Lorelei Clarke

There's a garden,

Full of hope and wisteria

Just outside the window

Guarded by thorns and frostbitten snow

In the garden,

Wild with the frenzy of a thousand dreams,

Bluebirds carry the wishes of lost souls,

Everything is found within the folds of the peonies.

Beyond the garden,

Snarls of doubt hide beside the path,

Dark skies rumble cries to those who listen,

A thousand directions that all point backwards.

But there's a garden,

Full of success and sunflowers

Just outside your window

If only you recall

That all thorns can do is draw blood.

Lorelei Clarke, is a teen American writer living in France. She takes inspiration from current events and issues she is passionate about as well as intimate personal experience.

RAVEN ON MY SHOULDER

By Kim Tennison

It all began beyond my understanding

When I was young and carefree

My raven perched upon my shoulder waiting

Was lingering and wordlessly relating

That it would always be integral part of me

Some days the raven I would barely notice

It hovered just beyond my sight and mind

It pecked my eyes and throat with force ferocious

It left me short of breath and feeling quite atrocious

Inside that strangest turmoil, I would feel confined

My body boiled with restless worry

My palms would sweat and thoughts compound

Emotions in my mind would come out blurry

For no one else could see my raven, or heard its sound

It seemed by its whims I was bound

Some named it shyness, others weakness

It morphed and fluttered but remained

And in confusion, I would dwell in my own meekness

Accepting my strange mindly bleakness

Afraid to further be disdained

I'd tried to lock away the raven

Or hide it at the very least

Imagined worlds and pen became my haven

In solitude, my mind was eased

Although I longed from those constraints to be released

Through ups and downs of trial and error

Past joys and sorrows we call life

I've tamed the raven, still the bearer

I hold for it no grudge nor terror

Of those thorns, I don't wish my being to be rife

I found compassion and acceptance

Learned others had their ravens too

Belief erased defeatist tendance

Retaining hope, through pain transcendence

Is what I yearn can come to you

Kim Tennison is passionate about human expression through creativity, She loves Terry Pratchett's Discworld series and Golden Retrievers. She moved to the rainy island that is the UK from Eastern Europe years ago. Nature is her main inspiration.

LOVE IS A FALLEN DOVE

By Neeve Milsom

All I want is the hope.

The freedom to believe.

To perceive the glistening future through rose coloured glasses.

To shield myself from a past so dark, no torch would ever cut through.

To watch as onyx blocks transform into gleaming pearlescent waves.

A true transition from dark to light, from never to always

An elaborate visage of collage lies hidden beneath the waves, layered and stacked up high.

Bursting through the glass ceiling, unperturbed, determined and infatuated.

But with the power, the demise of us all.

Fiery vengeance lurks in the shadows, awaiting, aching and hoping for more.

Awakening the suppressed secrets that haunt our souls.

Neeve is from Brighton in the UK. She finds writing poetry is a relaxing process which helps separate her from the chaos of modern life.

I SLEEP AND I SLEEP AND I SLEEP AND I
by Lewis Leverett

I sleep and I sleep and I sleep and I

I drag my eyes to the clock and examine the cost

I'm too tired to cry at the sleep I have lost

My neck does it ache and my head does it burn

I toss and I turn and I toss and I turn

And I toss and I turn and I toss and I turn

And my mind wants to think and my mind wants to learn

I think over every last bridge I must cross

I toss and I turn and I turn and I toss

Then I pick up my phone as the bedsprings dig deep

And I tell her about how I'm counting my sheep

But my neck does it ache and my head is still burning

I'm tossing and turning and tossing and turning

And tossing and turning and tossing and turning

The bags on my eyes are becoming concerning

She comes and I'm held and I don't count my sheep

And I sleep and I sleep and I sleep and I.

Lewis Leverett is a poet, screenwriter and singer-songwriter from Essex. In his poems and songs, Lewis enjoys manipulating rhythm and rhyme to explore truthful stories in a uniquely playful way.

DARLING

By Goda Buikute

Darling,

I became your poison Oleander, the forbidden bloom,

As my hellfire burnt your fragile skin and put you in gloom,

I promised I would never hurt you again till my nails turned blue,

But my bones sang deeply with a chorus of ghosts in unison,

'The greatest loves are doomed',

So, you buried me in Grace,

In Death, my spirit sang in shame,

My wounded heart, my broken mind,

My pearly tears lit by the moonlight,

My writhing soul stuck in the night,

My fingers dance on pages you left behind,

Your shadow hands still grip my guts,

I lay bare on shards of bone and memories turned to dust,

They coat my skin as ashes,

Ashes,

The soot stains my teeth till I bite for a kill and leave gashes,

Your truth is not in my memory,

(Wounds in your heart).

You left no warning signs for me,

(I ran from the start),

You gave me all you had,

(I gave you all I could),

You took all of it back,

(I fell as soon as your words stabbed my back).

Your whispers and smiles haunt my memories,

Memories,

Your broken promises and honey-soaked words lay in the hardened ground,

Your golden hands and deadly soul I have unravelled to understand,

The poison has leeched into my mind and my hands,

I lay in my coffin and pray for the ending of our Kingdoms' lands.

Goda lives in London and will soon start a creative writing course at a university by the south coast. Goda likes cats, poems, and picking ripe fruit from the garden during the summer months.

A LETTER FROM PERSEPHONE

By Alexia Schauer

When I leave,

do not think of me as anything but grateful

that I saw the Earth as the land

of vast glorious mountainous splendor.

Remember me by its cerulean sky, its clouds that lie lazily above

the butterflies—their wispy wings catching a ride on the

winds that sprawl over plains and caves and into the sea

which breaths calmly…tranquilly…

so stilly you can only faintly hear the brine whispering across

the sand.

When I leave,

do not be scared when the sea restlessly

churns and darkens and throws itself against the crag,

when winter's army stabs the wind

when the butterflies shrivel

when the vast glorious mountainous splendor

becomes a desert of winter.

Please, do not be scared when the Earth I so much loved

drains of color,

when the trees sag,

when the flowers wither,

when you look around and see but splinters

of some forgotten place and I am not there to offer my arms

and embrace you and tell you,

Mother, you cannot know to love the sea and the sky

if they are always blue and kind;

You will not know a butterfly is soft unless you have kissed a rock

Nor that honey is sweet unless you have sucked a bitter orange;

Winter is not so cruel when Spring is promised.

You must know before I go

Spring will always rise again,

and when that first bloom uncurls from the ground and stains

what once was white and wicked,

you will sob and fall to your knees

and breathe in the sweet nectar of Spring

for which you never noticed the smell of before.

That is where I will be, my loving Mother,

hibernating with Spring,

waiting to repulse winter

and yet again be with thee amongst the golden pansies,

-Persephone

From Atlanta, Georgia, USA, Alexia Schauer has had short stories published in a school magazine and an international literary journal. Alexia draws inspiration from nature and spends all her time outdoors.

THERE'S PEACE IN PROSPERITY
By Hannah Robinson-Wright

This is the mantra:

'For when I retire'

A house overseas,

A cottage in a shire.

A bucket list to conquer,

Filled with things the eye must see.

A hopeless believer,

As gullible as you or me.

For now, you are useful – they'll take you for all you've got.

When old bones go brittle,

They'll say you've had your lot.

But you are the lucky one,

For you got to see.

The years I spent preparing

for something that never came for me.

Hannah Robinson-Wright is a poet from Huddersfield in the UK who focuses on portraying working class culture in fiction. She is inspired by the likes of Tony Harrison and Stevie Smith.

THE DISHES ARE CLEAN

By Eiman Anwar

Sponges soaked in water

With soap squirted

Then squashed and squeezed,

Dishes scrubbed and cleaned.

Stubborn stains all washed and gone

Under running water until there's none.

The plates are dripping wet from their ritual washing

Then dried and wrapped in printed clothing.

Oh, look mother, how the dishes are clean!

Standing, shining in white so pristine.

From past stains purified, forgiven and forgotten

No questions asked of the food that was rotten.

But then there's us who fight for acceptance

With mistakes made for which there is no repentance.

Other times, an accusation is so badly believed

The innocent one is torn and tarnished but never freed.

Oh, look mother, how the dishes are clean!

But don't you remember the hands in which it has been?

Eiman Anwar is from: Manchester, UK. Poetry is the way in which he has always loved to unfold his thoughts on important issues on an individual, social and global scale.

GLANCING OVER PAPERBACKS

By Simeon Lumgair

A fleeting affinity, voyage through alluring realms

We were miles away, we were closer than love

A magnetic synergy, turning the silent page

Glancing above entrancing paperbacks

Drawn away by the rushing carriage

Strangers caught in an endless aeon.

Simeon is an award-winning writer based in London. He has written several screenplays and TV series and lyrics for songs. He has had his work featured in over 50 international festivals.

FLYING ENVY
By Olya Carter

I desire butterflies, I am a moth.

Helios emerged, a fainting spell forevermore.

I fly wistfully in a deep black, full of shining stars, sky

and a smile, a waning crescent moon.

Getting vanished in the mornings in the far distance.

At least my shadow reminds me my existence.

Monster should be my first name, I make it my last

but still there is a grain of envy in my palms.

Put me in the spotlight I will be natural.

Trying to linger wherever it shines the most even though I am nocturnal.

Olya lives in Athens, Greece. She has been writing poetry since she was very young. For her, poetry is all about romance, nature, beauty, expression, fantasy, creativity, love, all the tiny or huge things that we stay alive for.

SPEAKING TO MY FATHER, SPEAKING TO MY MOTHER

By Luigi Coppola

**(Set to music at *https://youtu.be/I_twWtHgd_A)*

Speaking to my father has become

not quite what is said, not quite not

but more than what isn't said

and much more than what is.

Speaking to my mother has recently become

The comfort of a cold, hollow point

Made warm and full and rounded

The way everything used to seem to be

The reassurance of continuance:

the old town unchanged, the weather

forgettable, the plans made

for a tomorrow that never comes.

Some life someplace is all that matters.

Stay, my father, my mother, in that time held

in place, a place that is closed now, safe, but once,

just one time, opened so I could leave.

Luigi Coppola is a teacher, poet, first generation immigrant and avid rum and coke drinker. Bridport Prize shortlisted, Ledbury and National Poetry Competition longlisted, Poetry Archive Worldview winner's list, publications include Worple Press' 'The Tree Line', Acumen, Ink, Sweat and Tears, Iota, Magma, Rattle and Rialto (read more at LuigiCoppolaPoetry.blogspot.co.uk).

AIRPORT SECURITY

By Charlie-Mai Dixon

We exist somewhere along the rope that ties

land to land, to land somewhere within

a land that doesn't belong to us.

Time is tangled around itself, where we are

It no longer fits into its own hands.

We write poetry at midnight,

and order pasta for breakfast.

They're over-charging, but we will hold

out our paper cups, nonetheless.

They fill them with hot water that tastes like

a delayed train, or a page's folded corner.

It's 5am, and we're watching the windows fog over.

We're watching the buildings shrink in on themselves.

Ashamed, as if you could be suddenly aware of insignificance.

They're drowning in our paper cups,

and we could hold the whole world in our hands

Charlie-Mai is a writer from North-East England. Having just completed his undergraduate degree, he is new to poetry and eager to explore and challenge the boundaries of structure and form.

SWALLOWED

By Imogen Smith

I can't swallow

The tears desperately shed

By bruised flesh

And stifled breath

Anemic footsteps on charnel ground

Splintered by godlike forces

The hallowed hand that wields the sacred instruments

Cutting down into unblighted graves

Of deadened strangled prayers.

Imogen is from Southampton in the UK and she writes to come to terms with the strangeness and ever-present horror of human existence.

JASMINE

By Stephen Kingsnorth

The greys and browns are all around,

but lightning stars of yellow strike

to break monotony of rime

that seals the prevalence of death.

How dare these petals risk the sharps,

some flimsy tissue crepe in sun;

what permit issued, warmer time,

appearance counter winter prime?

At least the lauded snowdrop bells -

supposed as signs of season's turn -

present a thick waxed hardened shell,

break crystals blanket, ready dressed.

Yet here against the honeyed blocks

these sparkles brighter than the stone;

this Roman candle shower, stark

amidst the loom of bitter pall.

A magic carpet, hanging wall,

the Persians thought a gift from God;

but where the flaw, one thread bare missed

as blossom tides us to the spring?

This contradiction to the norm

is what declares the globe a place

where unexpected signs of grace

invade the drab, and real can change.

Stephen Kingsnorth, retired to Wales from ministry in the Methodist Church due to Parkinson's Disease, spends innumerable hours writing poetry on the laptop, and has had pieces published by on-line poetry sites, printed journals. His blog is at https://poetrykingsnorth.wordpress.com

BUT YOU'RE STILL HERE

By Zara Shafique

I feel your words every night when I try to fall asleep,

And I follow the advice you gave when I start to panic,

And I see your face in the calm flow of the river,

And for a second it feels like you're still alive,

And then I realise, you're gone but you're still here.

I hear your voice in the wind on our hill,

And I hear your laugh every time I complete an essay,

And I remember your thoughts when I think of school,

And for a second it feels like you're alive,

And then I realise, you're gone but you're still here.

I think of you when I run in the crisp, cold mornings,

And I remember you in the delicate sounds of a piano,

And I feel your presence when I mediate the way you taught me,

And for a second it feels like you're alive,

And then I realise, you're gone but you're still here.

I see the essence of you as I walk through the streets we once walked through together,

And I remember your movements as I walk past your house,

And I can hear your breathing when I do the breathing techniques you taught me,

And for a second it feels like you're alive,

And then I realise, you're gone but you're still here.

I see you within the pain of my own eyes,

And I see your reflection in every tear of mine that spills.

However, this time I know you're not alive. I know you're gone.

But you're still here.

Published in 2022 by

The Anansi Archive

The Anansi Archive is an online community of writers supporting each other's literary endeavours.

If you would like to join this project please email

info@anasiarchive.co.uk

or visit the website at

www.anansiarchive.co.uk

If you have enjoyed this book, tell others about us.

Get the word out.

Printed in Great Britain
by Amazon